The Gift of Self
in Marriage

'People today listen more willingly to witnesses than to teachers, and if they do listen to teachers, it is because they are witnesses.'

Address to Members of the Concilium de Laicis (2 October 1974, quoted *in* Pope Paul VI, *Evangelii Nuntiandi*, Catholic Truth Society, London 2002, § 41. (I have modernised the wording slightly).

The Gift of Self in Marriage

A study of the mutual gift in the act of love in the light of the teaching of the Catholic Church and contemporary thinking and practice

Anita Dowsing

GRACEWING

First published in 2007

Gracewing
2 Southern Avenue
Leominster
Herefordshire HR6 0QF

ISBN 978 0 85244 155 8

Cover: Icon of The Marriage at Cana courtesy of
INTERAMERICAN Greek Life Insurance Company

Typeset by Action Publishing Technology Ltd,
Gloucester GL1 5SR

Contents

Notes

Bible quotations are taken from *The New Jerusalem Bible*, Standard
Edition, Darton, Longman & Todd, London, 1985 unless otherwise stated.
Abbreviations used for books of the Bible are as cited in *The New
Jerusalem Bible*.
Web addresses were current at the time of writing.

Acknowledgements

Many people have helped to shape this book and I am grateful to all of them, but I would like to thank the following in particular:

Archbishop Peter Smith, then Bishop of East Anglia, read my early, tentative plans and encouraged me to go ahead. Fr Simon Blakesley, VJ gave generously of his time to discuss aspects of canon law.

My three 'readers', Mrs Jane Powell, Mrs Cynthia Robinson and Rev Tony Ranzetta commented on each chapter as I, slowly, produced them and made sure that I stuck to my theme and said what I really meant.

Ruth Burrows (Sr Rachel of Quidenham) and Professor Margaret Spufford have read individual chapters and I have benefited greatly from their insights and comments.

I would also like to thank Tom Longford of Gracewing Publishing who helped extract a much better book from the manuscript I originally submitted.

My husband, Roy, has lived with this book for a number of years, always encouraging and focusing me as well as helping me with the many practical tasks associated with the writing. The book would not have been written without his constant support.

Finally, I am grateful to the following publisher for permission to quote from the copyright material below:

Darton, Longman & Todd, Ltd, *The New Jerusalem Bible*, Standard Edition, London 1985.

Anita Dowsing

Foreword

The institution of marriage has received some very hard knocks over the past forty years and today is under serious threat. The increasing number of divorces, the increasing number of people who cohabit rather than marry, and the legal recognition of civil partnerships for same sex couples, have done nothing to support or strengthen the institution of marriage, nor have they helped people understand the marital relationship as a vocation.

We Catholics don't live in isolation from the society of which we are members, and inevitably we are affected to a greater or lesser extent by the behaviour and attitudes of those around us. Our faithfulness to the teaching of Christ and His Church, which is demanded by our discipleship of Jesus Christ, can so easily be eroded by the relativist approach to truth which is so evident in our time.

Anita Dowsing's second book on marriage, *The Gift of Self in Marriage*, is a moving 'wake-up' call to all of us Catholics, and especially those who are considering entering marriage, or are concerned with preparing couples for marriage, or who have a role in helping those whose marriages are suffering strains and tensions.

She writes from her own experience and reflection as a married woman over the years, drawing on the Gospels, the teaching of the Church, the saints and eminent thinkers through the ages. Her aim is to draw us back to a fuller understanding of marriage as the committed gift of self of a man and a woman in a lifelong covenant of unconditional love. She is well aware of the forces in society which have made this more difficult over recent years and doesn't sidestep difficult questions. Whilst holding firmly to the truths of the faith embedded in the Gospels and the authoritative teaching of the

Church, her approach is wise, compassionate and inspiring.

Readers will find in this book much to reflect upon, and through the topics and questions for discussion at the end of each chapter, will be helped to understand in a balanced way the teaching of the Church and the practical wisdom of that teaching for the health of the institution of marriage and for those who are called to this wonderful vocation in life.

+ Peter
Archbishop of Cardiff

Preface

Motivation for Writing and Readership

When I was writing my first book, *A Marriage in Our Time*,[1] someone asked me, 'So what have you said about the Church's attitude to sex in connection with marriage?' 'I haven't said anything', I replied. 'It didn't fit in'. I still think that is true, but it is also true that I was immensely relieved to find that these topics did not go with the rest of the book. I was very much hoping that I would not have to write about these difficult and controversial topics in the future either. Then someone else said to me, 'I cannot explain the Church's teaching on marriage and sexual morality to my children. It makes no sense to them at all, and, if I'm honest, I feel a bit confused myself too. Why don't you write about this?'

And so the niggling began and was added to in my own mind, as I saw the widening gap between church teaching on some of these matters and the practice of many people, including Catholics. I realised that I could not escape writing about it, that, in fact, I wanted to make a personal statement about living with the Church's teaching in today's world to help others as well as myself, and so I began to write.

Limitation of Subject

My original intention was to cover those areas of sexual morality relating to the gift of self in marriage where the teaching of the Church and the behaviour of a significant number of Catholics differed widely, that is, premarital sex, contraception and second marriage after divorce.[2] (I decided to exclude any specific treatment of abortion, since I consider that a separate subject).

However, no marriage is lived in isolation from the society in which the spouses find themselves. In order to get a complete picture of the social context in which Catholics live their marriages today, it was also necessary to consider recent developments affecting marriage in society at large. These include new discoveries in the fields of biotechnology and embryology and the ethics associated with their use, as well as the interaction between human reason and religious faith, where these impinge on marriage. Although these areas of knowledge do not affect all married couples directly at present, they are important for a full understanding of the gift of self within Roman Catholic thinking and practice. The book therefore also provides a sketch of the relevant scientific and religious backdrop against which marriage is lived today.

Since the book is about marriage, it does not treat of homosexual relationships. This is not because homosexual people are of less value than other people, but because of the nature of marriage itself, as a mutual gift between a man and a woman.[3]

I have drawn on my own experience of married life, on conversations with others and also my reflection on the teaching of the Catholic Church on the gift of self in marriage over the years. The book is addressed to those, both Catholics and others, who find the Church's teaching on the sexual morality of marriage incomprehensible, unliveable and, in many cases, irrelevant, as well as to those who would like to deepen their present understanding of church teaching.

The book is therefore not an academic book, rather, it seeks to bridge the gap between the teaching of the Church and the practice of many of its lay members. It does so by considering the background for the contemporary assumptions about sex and marriage, which form the context in which Catholic teaching is now situated, and by explaining that teaching in a way that can make sense to ordinary people.

Geographical Limitations

Most if the material used in this book is based on the 'Western' scene, that is Western Europe and, to some extent,

North America, Australia and New Zealand, but much of what is discussed will, of course, apply to marriages involving Catholics, and other Christians, anywhere.

Arrangement of Chapters

The book is divided into three parts: the first, consisting of chapter one, sets the scene for the current dissociation of church teaching from the way most people live, the second, consisting of chapters two to four, provides the social and religious context for the main topic and the third, consisting of the remaining chapters of the book, reflects on the meaning of the gift of self in marriage today.

Assumptions of Prior Knowledge

I have assumed some familiarity with the Catholic and Christian 'scene', but little in the way of technical theological language. Any terms that might be unfamiliar to the general reader have been defined where they occur.

Who is the Book for?

The book is aimed primarily at those considering marriage, lay people involved in marriage preparation and support, as well as those already married, but it is my hope that parish clergy will also read the book, as a practical aid to preparing couples for marriage and caring for them and their families afterwards.

How to Use This Book

Each chapter is followed by a Summary and a List of Further Reading and Questions for Discussion are included at the end of the book. The book is thus suitable not only for the individual reader, but also for discussion groups and for use in connection with marriage preparation at parish, deanery or diocesan levels.

Notes

1 *A Marriage in Our Time, When Believer Meets Non-Believer*, Sheed and Ward, London 2000.
2 See chapter one.
3 *Catechism of the Catholic Church*, Geoffrey Chapman, London 1994, §§ 2357–2359.

Part One:

Introduction

Chapter One

Sex and Marriage: The Gap Between Catholic Teaching and Common Practice

*Can marriage be proclaimed as 'good news', as gospel living? ...
Or will generations to come simply laugh incredulously at such
notions?*

Clare Watkins[1]

*Mercy and faithfulness have met;
justice and peace have embraced.
Faithfulness shall spring from the earth
and justice look down from heaven.*

Psalm 84[2]

The year 2004 was the tenth anniversary of the International
Year of the Family. It was also the year in which the bishops
of England and Wales decided on a new initiative to listen to
the experience of marriage and family life of ordinary people
in every diocese.

Needless to say, the Church's teaching on sexual morality
was high on the agenda, especially with regard to its rejection
of contraception and sex before marriage. Three comments
from the final meeting in my diocese have stayed with me,
each one reflecting a different attitude:

'Once you've learnt to live with Natural Family Planning
(NFP), you wouldn't want anything else, and I wish someone
had spoken to me about it when we were being prepared for
marriage.' (NFP uses knowledge of a woman's fertile and infertile phases to achieve or avoid conception).

At the other end of the scale, someone said,

> 'You (the bishops) are not going to like this, but I think the
> Church is going to have to change over the issue of contracep-
> tion. After all, most women work now. They simply cannot
> have vast numbers of children. They want a life outside the
> home.' (She didn't say this, but of course the implication was
> that NFP did not 'work').

Another participant said,

> There's teaching on marriage and teaching on sex. If we're
> going to follow what the Church says, then we need to see the
> act of love as part of the whole picture of marriage.

The first two comments were expected, one representing the
smaller group within the Church who follows its teaching on
sexual morality, the other the much larger group who 'do
otherwise', at least in some respects, with a wide gap in
between. The third comment offered hope of bridging the gap,
I thought, because the speaker said, 'Tell us more, so that the
Church's teaching can make sense'. It also made the assumption that there was a 'more' to be told.

Marriage in Context

The gap between church teaching and the practice of many
Catholics in some areas of sexual morality reflects an even
wider gap between that teaching and the practice in society at
large. How does marriage fit into today's society?

Until not so long ago most people expected to get married
and to remain so till the death of one of the spouses. The
terms *unmarried*, *widowed* or, more rarely, *separated* or
divorced, all described a person's situation in life with reference to their marital status. *Marriage* meant sharing the whole
of life, it meant giving oneself in the sexual act and founding
a family. The word *single*, in the sense of an unmarried individual, contrasted with *couple*, meaning a man and a woman
who were married to each other.

On the other hand, the present fluidity of 'live-in relationships' was brought home to me forcibly last year, when I was asked to fill in a questionnaire with boxes like 'living alone', 'living with children', 'living with partner', but no box for 'married'. If marriage has become an optional extra to 'coupledom', at any rate in some people's consciousness, it is not surprising that there is confusion about exactly what marriage is, and hence also about the meaning of the mutual gift in the act of love.

Marriage 'in the Beginning'[3]

Old Testament

Marriage, linked to the physical gift of self between a man and a woman, has existed as long as there have been human beings around. The first account of Creation, at the beginning of the Old Testament, concludes with the creation of man and woman, made as lifelong gifts for each other, in the image and likeness of God.[4] This account describes how things were meant to be from the beginning, how it was intended for husband and wife to live with each other, in total fidelity. In spite of temporary departures from this model, faithful married love, as described, for instance, in the love poetry of the Song of Songs, was always held up as the ideal and as an image of God's love for his people.

New Testament: A Return to 'the Beginning'

When Christ discussed the question of divorce with a Jewish group called the Pharisees, he made it clear that the Old Testament prophet Moses permitted divorce only as a temporary concession to the 'unteachability' of the Israelites, and that it was not how marriage was meant to be 'in the beginning'.[5]

Indeed, in all his encounters with men and women, Christ pointed to the original order of Creation and showed them, with mercy and understanding, how each one could begin again, whatever their circumstances and I will return to this question in chapter five.

The Teaching of the Catholic Church

The Catholic Church has continued the teaching of Christ on sexual morality, but many people now consider this doctrine, certainly as formulated by the Church, to be harsh and unbending and without any real understanding of contemporary life. There is therefore a wide discrepancy between what the Church teaches, on many issues, and what a large number of people, including Catholics, choose to do.

On the other hand, the 'official' Church values sexuality and the sexual act in marriage highly, as can be seen from the beautiful description of the meaning of sex, in the document on the *Christian Family in the Modern World*:

> Sexuality, by means of which man and woman give themselves to one another through the acts which are proper and exclusive to spouses, is not something simply biological, but concerns the innermost being of the human person as such. It is realised in a truly human way only if it is an integral part of the love by which a man and woman commit themselves totally to one another until death.[6]

This mutual gift of the 'innermost being' presupposes a total commitment to the other person without any reservations or preconditions. In fact, the gift as described here is the gift as it was meant to be from the time of Creation and as Christ invites everyone to live it. This invitation comes to different couples at different stages in their lives, so that in many cases it becomes a chance to take the first step towards a new beginning in their life together. The Gospels are full of people making new beginnings and it is the Church's task to speak Christ's words of mercy, 'I don't condemn you. Go away and from now on, don't sin any more',[7] but also to remember what he said to Peter about how many times to forgive someone, 'I tell you, not seven times seven, but seventy times seven.'[8]

Marriage Trends

General

Government statistics for the year 2000 show that a majority of couples marrying in England and Wales now live at the same address before marriage, though that majority is considerably larger for those opting for a civil rather than a religious ceremony.[9] This difference may reflect the traditions of those belonging to non-Christian religions as well as the religious convictions held by some Christians. On the other hand, the typical age for first sexual intercourse both in Britain and in the US is now in the mid-teens, long before most people would consider marriage or even a stable cohabiting relationship.[10] Divorce rates are high both in Britain and the United States with a large proportion of the divorced in both countries remarrying.[11] The use of contraception inside and outside marriage is now taken for granted and there are many other ways in which the sexual act is separated from the conception of children. Both the Anglican and Methodist Churches accept the responsible use of contraceptives.[12]

Catholics

Clergy preparing couples for marriage can testify that premarital cohabitation is common among Catholics and I will return to this question in chapter five. There is evidence that marriages involving Catholics are almost as prone to breakdown as those of non-Catholics,[13] and that the incidence of remarriage after divorce among Catholics is comparable to that of the population at large,[14] with the consequence that the problems and pain of those involved is under constant debate within the Catholic Church.[15] The question of the use of contraceptives has become a private matter for many Catholics today.[16]

Closing the Gap

Accepting What People Do

Over the years civil legislation and, to a degree, regulations of some Christian churches, have sought to accommodate what couples actually did or wanted to do. Thus divorce has become relatively easy in many Western societies and remarriage in church of divorced people can take place both within the Methodist and Anglican Churches, though precise discipline differs between the two churches.[17]

There are now Christians who advocate the acceptance of pre-marital cohabitation as a step on the way to marriage. Thus the Anglican theologian Adrian Thatcher distinguishes between non-nuptial and nuptial cohabitation, with the latter being acceptable, in his view, because the couple intend to marry. The Catholic marriage specialist Jack Dominian takes a similar view, though with some reservations.[18] I do not think this distinction solves any problems, as it simply pushes the moment of decision back a step and, if the couple intend to marry, why not do so in the first place?

Since 1999 French law has permitted couples to marry 'Just a Little Bit', as one recent article described it. The idea is for a couple to have a *Pacte civil de solidarité (Pacs)*, which is a legal arrangement to be treated as a couple for the time being (by employers, for instance), but either party can end the *Pacs* at three months' notice. Some of the couples interviewed said that they expected to be together for a long time, but thought it dishonest to make a commitment they were not sure of being able to keep. Significantly, the article ended by stating that the *Pacs* fitted 'neatly with Europe's open aspiration to bring about a post-Christian society in which tradition and sacrament play no part'.[19]

Change and Development in Catholic Teaching

Since the liturgical changes following the Second Vatican Council (1962–65), there has been an expectation among

Catholics that other changes would follow and that these might include a revision of the Church's teaching on sexual morality. It is therefore important, even at this early stage in the book, to look at what kinds of change are possible within the Church and to consider the difference between fundamental doctrine, which cannot change, and the development or reformulation of doctrine which has occurred many times over the centuries and will continue to do so in the future.[20]

The document that accompanied the publication of the most recent *Catechism of the Catholic Church* made it clear how doctrine can be explained in new ways to meet new needs, while remaining faithful to the teaching that has been handed on since the time of the Apostles. I would therefore like to quote from the relevant passage:

> A Catechism should faithfully and systematically present the teaching of Sacred Scripture, the living Tradition in the Church and the authentic Magisterium [Teaching Office], ... It should also help to *illumine with the light of faith the new situations and problems which had not yet emerged in the past.*[21]

There is thus a continuous need to reflect on the full meaning of the Faith, so that it can speak to everyone, whatever their historic setting and culture and theologians and saints down the ages have all contributed to this shared reflection. The 'illumining' ('throwing light on' or 'clarifying') of new situations is one way of describing 'development in the Faith' and I will return to this question in more detail in chapter four.

Attitudes within the Catholic Church

As we saw at the beginning of this chapter, individual Catholics vary in their attitudes to the Church's teaching on sex and marriage. Some have no problem with it, others reject some of it, and yet others feel that the teaching needs to be presented in a way that takes into account the whole of married life rather than just its sexual aspects.

I think the main objections to the Church's teaching on sex are that it is out of date and out of touch and, worst of all, lacking in compassion for real-life people in real-life situations:

- 'Why shouldn't people live together before marriage?'
- 'Why can't people remarry after the breakdown of a first marriage?'
- 'Why shouldn't people be allowed to make love as often as they want to without fear of an unmanageable string of pregnancies?'

These are the kind of questions asked, with the implication that, in order to connect to the world as it is today, the Church must re-write the rule book. However, the rule book is based on the demands made by the full meaning of the act of love. These demands are difficult to keep, especially in today's society, which is why they must always be seen in the context of Christ's loving treatment of those who, initially, failed to live up to them, but were given a new chance through their encounter with him.

The Healing of Christ: Mercy and Justice Together

While writing this book, I have returned again and again to the Gospels and the way Christ treated people in all kinds of 'moral dilemmas'. He did not point to the rule book, saying, 'you are beyond the pale' (which would be justice without mercy), but nor did he say 'Right and wrong aren't absolutes. Perhaps in your situation what you did wasn't *really* wrong ...' (which would be mercy without justice). What he did do was to speak the truth in love, the whole truth about each person's situation, so that justice (putting matters right) and mercy (the chance to begin again) were inseparably joined together.

One of the best known examples of Christ's just and merciful approach can be seen in his parable about the Lost ('Prodigal') Son. After asking his father (God) for his inheritance in advance, the son leaves home to lead a dissolute life, squandering all his money and sleeping around. When he eventually comes to his senses, he decides to return to his father to ask him to take pity on him. 'Treat me like one of your hired hands', he says, 'I'm not worthy to be called your son'. Instead the father throws a party: 'My son has returned and all is forgiven. Let us celebrate!'[22] I will return to this story in chapter five, but here I simply want to point to the father's overwhelming forgiveness, which shows that there is always a way back, no matter where we have been.

In this book I have shared some of my own experience of living a Christian marriage as well as my growing understanding of the new Theology of the Body. This theology has put the mutual gift of the body, with all its spiritual significance, at the centre of married love and has therefore placed the act of love within the whole picture of marriage, as the participant at the 'Listening' meeting in 2004 had asked.[23] I believe that it is only by giving the act of love its rightful place at the centre of marriage that the gap between church teaching and the practice of many Christians can be bridged. Such bridge building will take time, but, as someone once said to me, 'It doesn't matter how slowly you move, as long as you move in the right direction.'

Summary

The basic definition of marriage in this chapter is a total, life-long and fruitful gift of self of one man to one woman. In the Catholic Church this gift between two Christians is seen as an image of Christ's gift of self to the Church and therefore as a gift in total and lifelong fidelity. Living the full implications of Christian marriage has always been difficult, but it has become particularly difficult in recent times, because the concept of marriage is questioned by many in contemporary society. This chapter describes the problems of many Catholics in connection with church teaching on premarital sex, contraception and second marriage after divorce. It outlines the ways in which practice, even within the Catholic Church often diverges from official teaching in these sensitive areas. After referring briefly to the teaching of other churches on these matters, the chapter points to the attitude of Christ to people in 'sexual difficulties', as the starting point for bridging the gap between church teaching and the practice of many Catholics, and others, today.

Further Reading

Dei Verbum ('Dogmatic Constitution on Divine Revelation'), in Vatican Council II, the Conciliar and Post Conciliar Documents, (ed.) Austin Flannery OP, Costello Publishing Company, New York 1984.
The whole question of 'handing on' the faith is treated in Chapter II.

John Paul II, 'Apostolic Constitution *Fidei Depositum'* in *Catechism of the Catholic Church*, Geoffrey Chapman, London 1994, p. 4, section 'Arrangement of the Material'.
A succinct description of the way in which faith develops, yet remains the same.

Duncan Dormor, *Just Cohabiting*, the Church, Sex and Getting Married, Darton Longman and Todd, London 2004.
Dormor argues for acceptance of pre-marital cohabitation by the Christian churches.

Michael Hornsby-Smith, *Roman Catholic Beliefs in England: Customary Catholicism and Transformation of Religious Authority,* Cambridge, Cambridge University Press, 1991.
This major study is based on research among 'ordinary' and 'core' Catholics in the 1970s and 80s. It shows how lay attitudes to sexual morality, especially with regard to contraception, have come to diverge from church teaching in the years since the Second Vatican Council (1962–65).

Liam Kelly, *Sacraments Revisited*, Darton, Longman and Todd, London 1998, pp. 156–66.

A good historical overview of the development of the sacrament of matrimony.

Notes

1 'Postscript: Witnessing to marriage', *in Priests & People*, vol. 18, no. 1, January 2004, p. 42.
2. *The Grail Psalms*, A New Translation, HarperCollins Publishers, London 1991.
3 Cf. Gn 1:1.
4 Gn 1:27.
5 Mk 10:4 and Dt 24:1, 3.
6 Apostolic Exhortation by John Paul II, *The Christian Family in the Modern World* (*Familiaris Consortio*), Catholic Truth Society, London 1981, § 11.
7 Jn 8:11.
8 Mt 18:21-22.
9 88.5% of men aged 30–34 (the largest numerical group) marrying in a civil ceremony in the year 2000 lived at the same address as their brides. The figure for the largest numerical group of women marrying in a civil ceremony in 2000 (25–29) was virtually the same (87.4%). The corresponding figures for those marrying in a religious ceremony were 59% for men and 55.2% for women. 'National Statistics, Census 2001, http://www.statistics.gov.uk /STATBASE/ssdataset.asp?vlnk=6156, Table 3.38. As 'straw poll' evidence, a survey carried out by the National Wedding Show in 2004 and reported in *The Times* 26 February 2004 showed that only 3% of the small number of participating couples were virgins on marriage and that 92% had lived together before marriage.
10 The median age for first intercourse in Britain, based on a survey between 1999 and 2001, was 16. 'Sexual behaviour in Britain: early heterosexual experience' by Kaye Wellings et al. in *The Lancet* vol. 358, Issue 9296, 1 December 2001, pp. 1843–50 (available online). The median age in the US in 1998 was $16^{1}/_{2}$. See *Family Planning Perspectives*, published by the National Family Planning and Reproductive Health Association July/August 1998 (available online).
11 According to *The Times*, 19 February 2003, quoting British 2001 Census and US Census Bureau, *c*.40% of British marriages end in divorce, with over a third of divorced people remarrying. In America half of all marriages end in divorce, with three-quarters of divorced persons remarrying.
12 For Church of England and Methodist teaching on contraception, see http://www.cofe.anglican.org/info/socialpublic/smte.html

#contraception and http://www.request.org.uk/issues/topics
/abortion/abortion07.htm.

13 In 1994 the divorce rate involving Catholics in the UK was
   c.75% of the general divorce rate and in the US it was *c*.80%.
   Melissa Wilde, 'From Excommunication to Nullification: testing
   and Extending Supply-Side Theories of Religious Marketing with
   the Case of Catholic Marital Annulments' in *Journal for the
   Scientific Study of Religion* 2001, pp. 235–49, table 2. See also
   Michael Hornsby-Smith, *Roman Catholic Beliefs in England:
   Customary Catholicism and Transformation of Religious Authority*, p. 183, which reaches the same conclusion, based on a 1978
   national UK survey.

14 In 1994 42% of ever divorced Catholics in the UK were remarried,
   whereas the figure for the US was 31%. See Melissa Wilde, 'From
   Excommunication to Nullification: testing and Extending Supply-
   Side Theories of Religious Marketing with the Case of Catholic
   Marital Annulments', pp. 235–49, table 2. The general remarriage
   rate in Britain in 1991 (the nearest comparable year for which
   evidence is a vailable) was *c*.36%. See *National Statistics Online*,
   http://www.statistics.gov.uk/CCI/nscl.asp?ID=7534, table 4:
   'Marriages by previous marital status and manner of solemnisation, 1991, 2001 and 2002'.
   I am grateful to my husband, Dr Roy Dowsing, for helping me
   with the interpretation of the Melissa Wilde data.

15 See chapters ten and eleven.

16 According to the Alan Guttmacher Institute 'Facts in Brief' on
   Contraceptive use in the US posted on the Web 2004, only 2.3%
   of women used 'periodic abstinence' as a method of family planning. (Data from the most current available. All data from
   research conducted by the A. G. Institute and the National
   Center for Health Statistics. http://www.agi-usa.org/pubs
   /fb_contr_use.html.)
   In the UK 1% of women using some form of contraception or
   family planning used the 'safe period' in 2002. UK Office
   for National Statistics, Table 10.1 'Women aged 16–49: trends
   in contraceptive use: 1986–2002'. http://www.dh.gov.uk
   /PublicationsAndStatistics/Publications/PublicationsAndStatistics
   Commenting on research carried out in the 1970s and 80s
   Michael Hornsby-Smith states that it was difficult for him to find
   any Catholic who wholeheartedly supported church teaching on
   contraception. See *Roman Catholic Beliefs in England: Custom-*

ary *Catholicism and Transformation of Religious Authority*, p. 171.

17 'The Church of England's Views on Issues in Human Sexuality', http://www.cofe.anglican.org/news and 'Methodist Conference 2002 Report': 'Marriage in the Methodist Church', Section II, http://www.methodist.org.uk/index.cfm?fuseaction=information.content&cmid=341. Even so, remarriage in a religious ceremony is rare. Thus, of the marriages solemnised in a religious ceremony in England and Wales in 2002 (*c.*33% of total), only about 7% were a remarriage for one or both partners. Of these some, of course, would have involved widows or widowers. See (UK) *National Statistics Online*, 'Marriages Solemnised and Manner', Table 4: 'Marriages by previous marital status and manner of solemnisation, 1991, 2001 and 2002'. http://www.statistics.gov.uk/CCI/nscl.asp?ID=7606.

18 Jack Dominian, *Let's Make Love*, Darton Longman and Todd, 2001, p. 108 and Adrian Thatcher, *Marriage after Modernity*, Sheffield, Sheffield Academic Press, 1999.

19 Fay Weldon, 'Will You Marry me ... Just a Little Bit?' in *The Times*, 12 May 2004.

20 'Dogmatic Constitution on Divine Revelation' (*Dei Verbum*), in Vatican Council II, the Conciliar and Post Conciliar Documents, (ed.) Austin Flannery OP, § 8.

21 Pope John Paul II, 'Apostolic Constitution *Fidei Depositum*' in *Catechism of the Catholic Church*, p. 4 (my Italics).

22 Lk 15:11–24, 31–32.

23 See chapter seven.

Part Two:
Married Love in Today's Context

Chapter Two

Time, the Fullness of Time, and Waiting

I charge you,
daughters of Jerusalem,
... do not rouse, do not wake my beloved
before she pleases.
Songs of Songs 3:5

His purpose he set forth in Christ,
As a plan for the fulness of time, ...
Ephesians 1:10[1]

Not so long ago I was talking to a Catholic friend whose son had just got married. He said, 'It's quite a business getting married, these days, you have to give six months' notice in our diocese!' But then he added, 'I suppose it's because the diocese doesn't want people to rush into marriage. It's a serious step, after all.' He was right, of course, marriage is a serious step, but when two people are in love, it is tempting to rush ahead, to take the next step, before they are ready for this.

In the Catholic Church (and many other churches too), marriage is a commitment for life, not something to be entered into lightly. It requires thought and careful preparation. The old saying, 'marry in haste, repent at leisure' is as true now as when it was first coined.

If a couple prepare for marriage as the Church expects them to and as some couples still do, there are two important periods of waiting before the marriage. There is the time during which they make the decision to marry, culminating in their engagement, and there is the time of the engagement, leading up to the wedding and the commitment for life expressed in the vows and physical gift of self. Both periods involve patient waiting for love to grow and mature and for its physical expression to match each stage of the couple's commitment to each other.

However, since instant gratification is now the common pattern in many areas of life, including the sexual one, the true value of the mutual gift of self is not so easy to understand, so that many couples do not see why they should wait to give themselves till they have made the lifelong commitment in marriage.

Waiting in Everyday Life

A friend who is a keen gardener once said to me, 'It's sad the way many people now just buy a plant in flower and throw it in the bin, once its flowering time is over. I like to grow things from seed and watch them grow and develop.' I agree with him, but there are all sorts of everyday situations where we still accept, where we have to accept, that waiting is part of the picture. To take an example, there is no way the process of wine making can be hurried or forced. If wine is drunk too early, it will not be good wine or not wine at all. All one can try to do is to create the right conditions for the wine to mature, to be ready for drinking – and the same is true of marriage.

The development of a loving relationship leading to marriage is above all about waiting, together, for the right moment to make the decision about a commitment for life. This 'right moment' cannot be 'summoned', rather, it is something that the man and the woman *receive*, when the wine is ready, in the fullness of time.

Time and the Fullness of Time

Greek, the original language of the New Testament, has two different words for time, *chronos* and *kairos*.[2] The former means time as a line of moments (English has borrowed the word in 'chronology'), the other means 'the fullness of time' or 'the right time'. In fact, the root meaning of *kairos* is a 'due measure' or a full measure, so that we have the basic idea of a vessel filling up. What is expressed in the Greek language therefore reflects a reality in life. Waiting for 'the fullness of time' is written into everyone's experience of life: the wine needs time to mature, so we have to wait. We keep pouring till the glass is full.

Yet, with the physical gift of self, which is the most fundamental and total gift anyone can give, there is often no willingness to wait, and to prepare, for the right moment. In much of contemporary attitudes and literature 'the fullness of time', the *kairos* for sex is 'when I want it'. There are therefore, as we have seen, many people who only discover the full meaning of the sexual act later in life and who are only then able to give themselves fully in the act of love.[3]

Waiting to Decide

Before she met her husband, a friend of mine had a boyfriend whom she was considering marrying. They had known each other for some time and there were many times when they, almost, got to the point of getting engaged. However, there was never a time when they were both certain at the same time. In other words, their *kairos* never arrived and both are now happily married to someone else.

Even with a relationship that eventually leads to marriage, love does not always grow at the same rate in the man and the woman. Loving someone nearly always involves patience and the ability to wait. If the couple have decided that the gift of self should take place only after they are married, this will call for a particular kind of patience, for them both.

Marriage and Waiting

The 'wait six months' requirement for engaged couples is in complete harmony with the nature of the marriage relationship. It is one way of saying that such a commitment needs careful thought and preparation. Since the couple have now decided to marry, one could see those last six months as the final testing time, and, hopefully, preparation, for their commitment. Waiting for the right moment to make love can teach a couple that love can endure, whatever the circumstances and this 'waiting as part of loving', is illustrated beautifully in the Old Testament Book called the Song of Songs.

Waiting in the Song of Songs

The Song of Songs, or the Song of Solomon as it is also called, describes in poetic language the mutual physical longing between a man and a woman and their waiting for each other and many couples will recognise what is described as part of their own experience.

The book begins very directly with the words of the woman (the *Beloved*),

> *Let him kiss me with the kisses of his mouth . . .*
> *delicate is the fragrance of your perfume,*
> *your name is an oil poured out . . .*[4]

Although the poems of the Song of Songs describe different aspects of love between a man and a woman, they do not tell a story as such and there is no clear distinction between the time leading up to the decision to marry and the time of engagement leading up to the wedding. Nevertheless there is a growing intimacy between the lovers, so that some of the earlier poems speak of the time before the marriage and some of the later ones assume that the marriage has been consummated.[5]

In all the poems there is an awareness that the couple need time for their love to develop, and the loving patience to wait for each other. In the poems describing the courtship, the man (the *Lover*) says three times,

> *I charge you,*
> *daughters of Jerusalem, ...*
> *do not rouse, do not wake my beloved*
> *before she pleases.*[6]

The *Beloved* is waiting for (or dreaming of?) the *Lover*,

> *My love thrust his hand*
> *through the hole in the door [to open the latch] ...*
>
> *I opened to my love,*
> *but he had turned and gone.*[7]

On the other hand, in some of the later poems, their love is described as consummated. The *Beloved* says,

> *I belong to my love and my love to me.*[8]

Put differently, this collection of poems from the Bible describes not only the time of waiting, but also the *kairos* moment for the marriage, the time of consummation.

Receiving the Moment

Waiting is part of living, but not all waiting is the same, because our waiting is coloured by the attitude with which we wait. Waiting for the *kairos* means attentively looking out for a moment that will be given and that will enable us to take the right next step in our lives.

For a believer, it means an acceptance that I receive my life and its events from God, not passively, but in willing cooperation with him. The experience of waiting and of looking for the *kairos* moments is particularly poignant in the man-woman relationship, but openness to what will come can become a way of life. In Christian thinking this attitude is shared with the whole of Creation, which is waiting, indeed 'groaning' as if in labour, for the final fulfilment of all things, on the last day, at the end of time.[9]

God's Waiting for Us

Waiting is hard and it is tempting to try to force the moment of fulfilment, to seek to control rather than to receive. However, as with every other aspect of human life, God is not asking us to do what he has not experienced himself, in some form, through his Son Jesus. Karl Rahner, the German theologian whose work has broken much new ground, has spoken of Christ's patient waiting for each one of us, through the centuries, as the long 'short' moment, which we like to call world history and our own lives.[10] Seen against this background, our waiting for the *kairos* moment of mutual gift in marriage takes on a wider perspective, which is made even more poignant through Christ's description of himself as the 'bridegroom' of the Church. The relationship between husband and wife in marriage thus gains strength from the relationship between Christ and the Church and I will return to this theme in future chapters.[11] For the moment, it is enough to bear in mind that God does not ask us to do anything without being there with us, giving us the strength to do it.

Forcing the Moment or Receiving the Moment

In the light of the full meaning of the gift of self in marriage, and of Christ's patient waiting for each one of us, the minimum time of preparation to get married, which my friend thought a little excessive, does not appear unreasonably long.

However, waiting for the right time and receiving the moment (the *kairos*) to act are concepts that go against the prevailing ideas in our times, when the ability to do something is often equated with the right to do it and it is this wider context for the gift of self that we must now consider.

Summary

Marriage is a commitment in time, while both spouses live. This chapter considers the meaning of waiting, patience and the fullness of time in the light of the biblical description of married love in the Song of Songs and in contrast with the instant gratification mentality of much of contemporary society.

Further Reading

Henri Nouwen, *The Path of Waiting*, Darton, Longman and Todd Ltd, London 1995.
Reflections on the meaning of waiting in everyday life.

Karl Rahner, SJ, *The Eternal Year* ('Christmas'), (tr.) John Shea, SS, Burns and Oates, London 1964, pp. 19–26.
Contains a profound reflection on God's waiting for mankind to respond his love.

Notes

1 Taken from the translation used in *Morning and Evening Prayer with Night Prayer* from *The Divine Office*, Collins, E. J. Dwyer, Talbot, London – Glasgow, Sydney, Dublin, first printed 1976, p. 1009. The compilers have used a number of different translations, but do not indicate which translation they have used in any given case. See p. 1175. The translation is not from the Jerusalem Bible.
The word *kairos* is used for *time* in the original Greek; 'fulness': *sic*.

2 *An Intermediate Greek-English Lexicon*, founded upon Liddell and Scott's Greek-English Lexicon, Clarendon Press, Oxford 1955.

3 See especially chapters one, five and twelve.

4 Sg 1:2-3.

5 *The New Jerusalem Bible*, 'Introduction to the Song of Songs', p. 1029.

6 Sg 2:7 and 3:5, 8:4.

7 Sg 5:4, 6.

8 Sg 6:3.

9 Rm 8:22.

10 Karl Rahner, SJ, *The Eternal Year* ('Christmas'), p. 23.

11 See especially chapters eight and thirteen.

Chapter Three

Science and Sex: Discovering or Controlling Creation

In the person whose mind is sound there is no need for letters,[the only book he needs] is the nature of God's Creation: it is present whenever I wish to read his words.

St Antony of Egypt[1]

Science and theology ... share one fundamental aim ... in their different ways and in their different domains, each is concerned with the search for truth.

John Polkinghorne[2]

We live in times of a scientific knowledge explosion, much of it in the field of reproductive science and technology and new scientific discoveries always carry with them a responsibility for how they are used. In the past, for instance in connection with the splitting of the atom and the consequent bomb-making potential, this responsibility was carried by a relatively small number of people, that is, the scientists involved in the new discoveries and the politicians who, eventually, decided to use the atomic bombs.

The responsibility for the use of the new scientific discoveries in the fields of reproductive science and technology is shared by a much larger number of people, ranging from research scientists, to legislators, to members of the governmental agencies controlling the use of the new discoveries, and, significantly, ordinary men and women deciding whether and how to apply this knowledge in their own lives. The teaching of the Church on the proper application of scientific discoveries is of new practical significance to a large number of lay people in our times.

Although I cannot claim any specialist knowledge of bioethics or of the ethics of the application of scientific discovery in general, I think it is necessary to look at these matters in outline, because they form the context in which ordinary Catholics, and many others, make some of the most important decisions of their lives.

The Use of Scientific Discovery

For a reputable scientist the motivation for any research programme is the desire to find out how things work, that is, to discover the truth about them, and in most fields of knowledge he or she does not know at the outset what they will find. It is only when they come to the application of their new discoveries that scientists begin to realise their potential for good or evil, as was the case in relation to the splitting of the atom in the past and in our own times in relation to the discoveries of reproductive science.[3]

Splitting the Atom

In the early 1940s the newly discovered capacity to split the atom made possible the manufacture of an atomic bomb. In July 1945 Leo Szilard and a group of sixty-nine other scientists involved in nuclear research sent a petition to President Roosevelt reminding him of the terrible consequences of any use of the atomic bomb on Japanese cities. The letter warned that a nation which employed these newly liberated forces of nature for purposes of destruction might have to bear the responsibility of opening the door to an era of devastation on an unimaginable scale.[4]

As we know, the warning was not heeded and atomic bombs were dropped on Hiroshima and Nagasaki and such bombs continue to present a danger to the existence of us all. The splitting of the atom carried with it a challenge to the contemporary ethical norms, which most people could not immediately comprehend.

Using What We Know

It is said that the co-pilot of the plane which dropped the first atomic bomb on 6 August 1945 looked down in horror, saying 'My God! What have we done!'[5]

After Hiroshima, Szilard gave up physics and turned to biology, persuading others to do the same. In his view, it was high time to apply able minds to research into life and particularly human life.[6] However, the problem of the application of scientific knowledge did not go away, as can be seen from the fact that, a couple of generations later, we are faced with exactly the same fundamental problem that Szilard and his colleagues wrestled with in relation to the atomic bomb: 'What does our new scientific knowledge enable us to do?' 'What are the potential consequences of doing what we can do?' and 'How do we know what it is right to do?'

The Anglican physicist and theologian John Polkinghorne has described the dilemma well when he said that

> The ethical snare for the scientist is to get so caught up in the excitement of research that there is never time to ask where it is going and to what end. Not everything that can be done should be done.[7]

This is true in particular in relation to the use of the many new discoveries in reproductive science and technology.

Reproductive Technology and the Gift of Self in Marriage

The new discoveries in reproductive science and technology can be used in ways that strike at the heart of the mutual gift of self in marriage. Technological and chemical methods of avoiding conception have been available for a long time, but new technological means of avoiding or achieving conception are currently being discovered at such a rate that it is difficult to keep pace with, let alone understand, all the new developments and their use in human fertilisation and embryology.

The fertilisation of a human egg can now be done *in vitro*, that is, in a glass dish in the laboratory. The implantation of a fertilised egg can be carried out through medical intervention and eggs and sperm from people other than the couple seeking to have a child can be used.

Although legislation exercises some control over what is permitted in civil society in terms of fertilisation and foetus implantation, many practices are now commonplace, which would have been assigned to the wilder realms of science fiction not so many years ago.[8] To give some examples:

> In some parts of the world sperm banks now exist, which are used in a number of different ways, depending on the legislation of individual countries. If it is foreseen, for instance, that a man will become infertile, his sperm can be stored in order to inseminate his wife or partner at a later date. In such cases the child is, of course, genetically that couple's child, but sometimes the use of frozen sperm is taken a step further, so that it is donated, or even sold, for the use of any woman who wants a child but not a married or co-habiting relationship. There can be many different motivations for such an action, but one cannot exclude what a friend of mine once called the 'I want it, it's mine' attitude. A child conceived in this way is deprived of a father, not through misfortune, but through the misguided actions of its mother and the sperm 'donor'.
>
> The term *surrogacy* is used to describe an arrangement whereby a woman bears a child for a couple unable to have a child of their own, either by inseminating the woman with the father's sperm, or by implanting an embryo into the surrogate mother's womb. The possibilities for confused emotions and loyalties for all those involved in such an arrangement (not least the child when it grows up!) are obvious. The fact that the bond between mother and baby is not so easily broken can be seen from the number of cases in which the surrogate mother has wished to keep the baby she has carried and given birth to.

I will return to some of these questions in chapters four and seven, but here I have described some extreme cases, which have already happened, to illustrate a point. There are undoubtedly situations where the motivation for procedures like those mentioned is altruistic rather than financial, so that the intention is to help infertile couples have a child they could not otherwise have. Nevertheless, the cases described highlight what it is we can already (and might in the foreseeable future) tamper with, through these new practices.

The interpretation of the gift of self in marriage, and its potential fruit in childbearing, depends, fundamentally, on how we see ourselves as human beings. If we regard our bodies and our children as commodities, which we can dispose of or trade with at will, aware only of the consequences that we ourselves can foresee, then the way is open to an increasing fragmentation of human relationships and of the reproductive aspects of the human body.

It is thought-provoking that in recent years some of the children resulting from donor insemination have begun to ask who their fathers are. A few years ago, in a test case brought by two donor offspring, a girl of six and a woman of thirty, the British High Court ruled that such offspring should be entitled to learn all they could about their biological fathers and mothers. After the case, the woman was reported as saying, 'This is an important and heartening event on a long road to recognition of us as people – just like everyone else, with social and genetic roots – rather than as *products*.'[9] Many countries, including, since 2005, Britain, now allow donor offspring access to the identity of their genetic parents once the children reach a certain age.[10]

The wish to know where you have come from is justifiable both from an ethical and a practical point of view, but I think it goes deeper than that. It surely expresses a desire to belong to a family with a father and mother and to be the result of their loving mutual gift. This desire tells us something important about the ethics of applying new scientific discoveries to concrete human situations. The misuse of the discoveries about human reproduction and embryology has the potential to damage our world to an extent comparable to that of the splitting of the atom.

Church Teaching as a Standard for the Application of Scientific Discoveries

The great difficulty about moral and ethical choices in our times is that there is no generally accepted moral standard, so that actions that appear right to one person may be totally unacceptable to another. Without an absolute standard, how does the scientist, and the ordinary lay person using scientific discoveries, know what should or should not be done?

The *Catechism of the Catholic Church* states that

> Science and technology by their very nature require unconditional respect for fundamental moral criteria.[11]

It goes on to speak of research 'at the service of the human person' and 'in conformity with the plan and will of God'. It is a matter of seeking what is truly good for mankind and here science alone cannot provide an answer.

Two Different Attitudes to Research

The Danish Catholics among whom I grew up spoke of two different ways of studying the Bible. 'It was possible to consider it', they said, 'in a *sitting* or a *kneeling* way.' A *sitting* attitude meant that we approached the study of a biblical passage with the focus on our own ability and knowledge rather than on Scripture as God's Revelation. A *kneeling* attitude meant respect for the integrity of the biblical text and above all faith in the God who had inspired it as the starting points for any human interpretation.[12] In other words, there was a choice between putting ourselves in charge and treating Scripture as a gift from God's hand. I do not know where these two expressions come from, but I think they can equally well be used about the application of our present knowledge about human sex and reproduction.

A *sitting* attitude to the application of human reproductive science and technology implies that the scientist has assumed the right not only to analyse the material, but also to use the new knowledge in ways that fail to take account of the full truth about men and women as creatures. In this case, the scientist puts him or her self in the place of the Creator. If, for instance, a scientist uses his embryological knowledge to create a human embryo outside the womb, then he separates conception from the mutual gift of self of the father and mother. He is doing what he *can* do without taking full account of what it is *right* to do.

On the other hand, a *kneeling* attitude respects both the integrity of Creation and the intention of the Creator when he made us in this particular way and no other. The *kneeling* scientist might, for instance, apply his or her knowledge of the processes of reproduction to help a woman pinpoint her fertile and infertile phases, thereby enabling her to seek or avoid conception without fragmenting the act of love.

Both non-believers and believers can show the respect for the integrity of their subject that we have called *kneeling*. However, if this attitude is to be taken to its full potential, it needs to move from respectful interest in the subject under investigation to respect for and faith in its Creator. The believing scientist takes into account not only his or her own findings, but also looks for a God-given pattern in Creation, revealing the mind of the Creator.

The Whole Truth

In his document about the relationship between *Faith* and *Reason*, Pope John Paul II said that in their search for understanding of the world around them and of the functioning and meaning of their bodies 'men and women are on a journey of discovery which is humanly unstoppable'.[13]

The truth about the human body and its reproductive capacity which has been discovered by scientists and the truth about the human being expressed in God's Revelation support each other,

> It is the one and same God who establishes and guarantees the intelligibility and reasonableness of the natural order of things

upon which scientists confidently depend, and who reveals himself as the Father of our Lord Jesus Christ.[14]

There is therefore no real discrepancy between the findings of science and the findings of theology. The discrepancy comes in when one or the other discipline is used for a purpose for which it was not intended. Thus, for instance, reproductive science is not intended to step into the shoes of God the Creator, conceiving human beings outside the act of love, nor is theology intended to make statements about, for instance, astronomy. In her book *Galileo's Daughter*, Dava Sobel quotes Cardinal Cesare Baronio, a contemporary of Galileo's, as having said that the Bible was a book about how one goes to Heaven – not how Heaven goes.[15]

Revelation does not tell us about the structure of the human body, but it does tell us what it means to be human. In order to be fully human, we must study both Revelation and Creation and we need to use our growing knowledge about Creation in the light of God's Revelation.

Conclusion

As we have seen, in the honest and patient search for truth there is no fundamental difference of approach between the scientist and the theologian. It is primarily in the application of knowledge that different ethical stances make themselves felt. It seems to me that the *sitting–kneeling* difference is at the heart of the gap between many contemporary applications of reproductive discoveries, on the one hand, and the teaching of the Catholic Church about the gift of the human body, on the other. The danger of a reproductive science put to purely utilitarian use is that, by presenting as acceptable the separation of conception from the act of love, it will accelerate the fragmentation of the gift of self that is already in evidence in society today.

The details of research into embryology and fertility are difficult for the non-expert to understand, but it is possible for everyone to understand the gift of self as a total gift between husband and wife and therefore to make use of the findings of reproductive science only where these are compatible with the full meaning of the gift.

Summary

This chapter discusses the application of scientific discoveries with special reference to the use of discoveries in sexual and reproductive science. A contrast is drawn between two different attitudes occurring both in theological and scientific investigation. One of these is characterised by self-satisfaction and self-sufficiency, the other by humility and, in a believer, adoration. The two attitudes are discussed in relation to the difficult personal choices facing lay people today, as they decide how to use the options presented by the new discoveries in sexual and reproductive science.

Further Reading

John Paul II, *Faith and Reason* (Fides et Ratio), Encyclical letter to the bishops of the Catholic Church, Catholic Truth Society, London 1998, especially chapters III and IV.
Fundamental teaching on the search for truth and the relationship between faith and reason.

Jane Asher, *The Longing*, Harper/Collins, London 1997.
A novel which considers many of the negative effects of *in vitro* fertilisation. Based on research into the work of a gynaecology and fertility centre and interviews with women undergoing fertility treatment.

Nicholas Evans, *The Smoke Jumper*, Corgi Books, London 2002.
A novel, which looks at *in vitro* fertilisation in a more positive light, but illustrating the pitfalls too.

J. Polkinghorne, *Belief in God in an Age of Science*, Yale University Press, New Haven and London, 1998, especially chapters two, four and five.

A thought-provoking and readable book by a distinguished physicist and Anglican priest.

Notes

1 As quoted by William Dalrymple in *From the Holy Mountain*, Flamingo, an imprint of HarperCollins Publishers, 1998. p. 404. (First published in Great Britain by HarperCollins Publishers, 1997).

2 J. Polkinghorne, *Belief in God in an Age of Science*, pp. 99–100.

3 I am indebted to my husband, Dr Roy Dowsing, for throwing light on this problem.

4 'A Petition to the President of the United States', US National Archives, Record Group 77, Records of the Chief Engineers, Manhattan Engineer district, Harrison–Bundy File, folder #76.Transcription as e-text, copyright 1995–8 by Gene Dannen, http://www.dannen.com/decision/45-07-17.html

5 The Hidden and Deeper Legacy of Hiroshima; *THE HIROSHIMA TAPES*, as told by the psychotherapist of the Hiroshima Pilot. http://www.csi.ad.jp/ABOMB/index.html. The site refers to the book *LOOKING UP, LOOKING DOWN: The Psychology of the A-Bombers and Survivors of Hiroshima*, by Glenn Van Warreby. No place or date of publication, or page reference, given.

6 J. Bronowski, *The Ascent of Man*, Book Club Associates, London, 1976, p. 370.

7 J. Polkinghorne, *Belief in God in an Age of Science*, p. 92.

8 In Britain the watchdog for this whole area is the Human Fertilisation and Embryology Authority.

9 'Donor children "should be able to find fathers"' *The Times*, 27 July 2002. My emphasis.

10 *The Times*, 23 November 2005.

11 *Catechism of the Catholic Church*, Geoffrey Chapman, London 1994, § 2294.

12 That is, of course, not to say that we should not use our training and intelligence when studying the Bible.

13 John Paul II, *Faith and Reason (Fides et Ratio)*, Catholic Truth Society, London 1998, § 33.

14 Ibid., § 34.

15 Dava Sobel, *Galileo's Daughter*, Fourth Estate, London 1999, p. 65.

Chapter Four

Fragmentation and Clarification

The spirit of the Lord is on me,
for he has anointed me
to bring the good news to the afflicted.
He has sent me to proclaim liberty to captives,
sight to the blind,
to let the oppressed go free.

Isaiah 61:1-2[1]

This catechism will ... contain both the new and the old ...
because the faith is always the same yet the source of ever new
light.

Pope John Paul II[2]

In the last chapter I looked at some of the ways in which a misguided use of the discoveries of reproductive science and technology could lead to separation of the fruitful aspect of the act of love from the mutual gift of the spouses, so that the act was broken into fragments.

In this chapter I want to focus on the separation of the sexual act from commitment in marriage, which the development of effective contraception has made possible. I want to say something about the Church's teaching on the sexual act and how that teaching is seen from outside the Church. I will also outline some of the development in church teaching on marriage over the centuries, so as to show what is meant by development, and how development differs from change in doctrine. It will be important to bear this distinction in mind for the chapters dealing with contraception (seven) and second marriage after divorce (eleven), because there is a widespread expectation among Catholics that church teaching is likely to change in these areas. At the end of the present chapter I point to the Theology of the Body as a means of healing the fragmentation and incomplete understanding of the gift of self in marriage.

The Gift as a Fragment of the Whole

When I recently looked at an application form for a credit card, I noticed a new category under 'marital status', that of 'cohabiting'. It was the first time I had seen this as a category on an official form, though I have certainly noticed that hospital personnel now tend to refer to your 'partner' rather than your 'husband' or 'wife'.

There are many cohabiting and non-cohabiting relationships in which men and women make love. Though many people still see the act of love as a significant step in a relationship, it is by no means linked to marriage only, even as an ideal. 'The choice to make love is my choice', many people would say. 'It's my decision, and that of the person I make love to'. The changes in the behaviour of 'officialdom' thus reflect a change in attitude to sex in a large part of the general population.

What Does the Church Say?

In recent teaching the Catholic Church has defined the act of love as the definitive physical sign of the gift of self in marriage.[3] It is a total mutual gift of husband and wife to each other. The *Catechism of the Catholic Church* (1994) describes the act of love as 'noble and honourable' and sexuality as a 'source of joy and pleasure', and it goes on to quote words spoken by Pope Pius XII in 1951:

> The Creator himself . . .established that in the [generative] function, spouses should experience pleasure and enjoyment of body

and spirit. Therefore the spouses do nothing evil in seeking this enjoyment and pleasure. They accept what the Creator had intended for them.[4]

In my view it is precisely because of this re-emphasis on the goodness of all things physical that the Church can speak with conviction to people who agree with it on the basic goodness of sexual pleasure, but who think such pleasure can also have its place outside marriage.

The Church's Teaching on Sex as Seen from the Outside

The fact that the official teaching of the Church expresses such a positive view of sex will come as a surprise to many people outside and (dare I say it?) inside the Church. In a recent conversation about the Church's attitude to sex, a friend said to me, 'It's all very well saying that the Church now has this wonderful theology of the body. And you talk about the Song of Songs in the Bible as evidence that the sexual aspect of married love has always been valued, but that is not the impression I get.'

'Honestly', he went on, 'I wonder how many priests have ever thought highly of the sexual aspect of marriage. The message that I get from the Church' (he was brought up as a Catholic, but no longer practises) ' is that sex is not valued, even in the Church as it is now.'

This friend is by no means the only person who has expressed such views to me, yet the capacity for sexual plea-sure is God given. I am reminded of one of the art critic Sister Wendy Beckett's television programmes in which, comment-ing on a nude painting, she said something like, 'I don't believe that God averted his eyes while creating certain parts of the body!'

Official church teaching does not believe that either, but there has, from the earliest days been, shall we say, an under-current of thought within the Church, which looked at sex, even sex within marriage, as inherently suspect. It is significant, I think, that Pope Pius XII should have considered it necessary to say that sexual enjoyment is not evil and that the authors of the *Catechism*, some fifty years later, should have chosen to quote this particular passage. If the idea that sex is evil, or at any rate considered as such by the powers that be, had not been held by a considerable number of members of the Church, there would have been no need for such a forceful statement to the contrary.

Perceptions of Sex within the Church

This is not the place to attempt a history of the Church's attitude to sex in marriage through the ages, but I think it is necessary to mention some key factors in the development of attitudes to sex within the Catholic Church, because these can throw light on some of the present-day misunderstandings about church teaching.

Manichaeism

Pope John Paul went to the root of the problem when he explained that the negative attitude to the body, and hence to sex, originated with the influence on Christianity of Manichaeism, a fourth-century Eastern religious movement, which saw everything material, including the body, as evil. The influence of this movement spread throughout the Roman Empire and its effects on Christianity can be felt even now.[5]

St Augustine

The fourth-century theologian St Augustine argued against a positive view of sex in itself, because of the loss of self-control, which he saw as inherent in the sexual act after the Fall. Because of their disobedience to God, men and women were 'handed over to themselves' but could not be obedient to themselves either. The result was a loss of self control, especially in sexual matters.[6] For Augustine, the only justification for sexual intercourse was the fact that it was necessary for the continuation of the human race.[7]

St Thomas Aquinas

St Augustine's negative view of the pleasure associated with
sexual intercourse went largely unchallenged until the thirteenth
century, when St Thomas Aquinas rejected the point of view
that sexual pleasure was a bad thing in itself. In fact, for him,
sexual pleasure would have been even greater before the Fall,
since people would then have been purer and their bodies conse-
quently more sensitive.[8]

With regard to the 'excessive' pleasure associated with the
sexual act St. Thomas says, (surely with a smile!) that

> The abundance of pleasure which is in a sexual act ordered
> in accordance with reason is not contrary to ... virtue ...
> For it is not contrary to reason if the act of thinking is some-
> times interrupted by something which is done in accordance
> with reason; otherwise it would be contrary to reason for
> somebody to give himself up to sleep.[9]

St Francis de Sales

In the first guide to the spiritual life written specifically for lay
people, St Francis de Sales, who was Bishop of Geneva in the
seventeenth century, describes married love in all its aspects
with great tenderness and respect. For instance he says:

> Love and fidelity joined together always produce familiarity
> and mutual trust, and hence in their married life the saints,
> both men and women, have used many reciprocal caresses,
> truly affectionate, but chaste, tender, sincere caresses.[10]

In this description husbands and wives express their love for
each other in and through their bodies, not seeking pleasure for
its own sake, but seeking to give a physical 'voice' to the love
that binds them together.

Our Times: A Return to the Sources

Much renewal of Catholic thinking in recent years has been
linked to a return to biblical sources and to how things were 'in

the beginning'.[11] In the context of the act of love, this has meant a renewed awareness that God created man and woman and that he gave them the capacity for sexual pleasure in their mutual gift of self. In other words, there is recognition of the value of the body, which is particularly associated with the Theology of the Body developed by Pope John Paul II, and I will come back to this later.[12]

Fragment or Partly Lit Up?

Could one say that the Church's teaching on sex within marriage was fragmented in earlier centuries? I think it is closer to the truth to say that the 'return to the sources' has meant a return to what has always been there, but has perhaps been neglected or not fully understood.

Here I think we need a different image. One could look at the Church's teaching on the total gift of self in marriage as a painting with a light shining on it. There have been times when this light shone (almost) only on one part, the call to have children. In our times the light is also beginning to shine on the other part of the act: that of the mutual gift of self, accompanied by God given pleasure and joy.

Does that mean that, for many centuries the Church deliberately took apart what it knew belonged together? No; but one could say that over time the Church came to a fuller and clearer understanding of what the gift of self in marriage meant. It is this clearer understanding that Pope John Paul referred to when he spoke of the *Catechism* illumining new situations with the light of faith.[13] On a basis of this new light it became possible to draw conclusions about what had always been there, but was now revealed in greater clarity. This is how faith develops.

Development in the Faith

Growth in Understanding within the Church

Ever since the earliest days of the Church, people have reflected on the meaning of the revelation taught by Christ to the Apostles and handed down in the Church and they have drawn conclusions in the light of their own times and situations. However, the message taught by Christ remains the same, so, quite early on, theologians began to ask questions like the one posed by the fifth-century theologian Vincent of Lerins,

> Can there then be no progress of religion in the Church of Christ?

He answers himself,

> There is indeed much progress ... but true progress, not change ... growth in understanding, knowledge, and wisdom, ... but within the same dogma and meaning.[14]

This progress in 'understanding, knowledge and wisdom' comes about when, inspired by the Holy Spirit, the whole Church uses its God-given intellect to throw light on the teaching handed down in the Church and its application in daily life.

However, individuals can go wrong (the *Catechism* speaks of 'wounded human reason'[15]), so that it is the task of the teaching office of the Church (the *Magisterium)*, as exercised by the pope and the bishops to share in this reflection and guide it, to ensure that no material is introduced which is alien or contrary to the original revelation of Christ to the Apostles. When necessary, the *Magisterium* issues authoritative formulations of the faith, often in response to 'burning issues' of the times.[16] Thus, for instance, the encyclical *On Human Life* (*Humanae Vitae*), published in 1968, dealt with the controversial issues of the transmission of human life and of contraception and I will return to this document in chapter seven.

Thinking about the Faith: A Service to All in the Church

It is not only theologians who are called to think about the Faith and formulate it in new and more profound ways in response to the burning questions of a particular age. All Catholics, and indeed all Christians, have a duty to reflect on their faith and, where appropriate, to express their reflections in speech and writing.[17]

The *Catechism of the Catholic Church* says that:

> In the work of teaching and applying Christian morality, the Church needs the dedication of pastors, the knowledge of theologians and the contribution of all Christians and men of good will ... Thus the Holy Spirit can use the humblest to enlighten the learned and those in the highest positions.[18]

In this way the philosopher Edith Stein took the unusual step of writing to the then Pope (Pius XI), to warn him of the dangerous developments in Hitler's Germany.[19] It is thought that her letter influenced his anti-Nazi encyclical *Mit Brennender Sorge (With Ardent Concern)*, which he published in 1937.[20]

Closer to our own times, it is significant that two lay people were invited to address the Second Vatican Council in 1963, speaking in support of ecumenism and greater lay involvement in the Church.[21]

At a less public level every Christian is faced with questions of how to live their faith in everyday life. Sometimes these can lead to conflict between individual opinion and church teaching and nowhere is this more true than in relation to the Church's teaching on sexual morality.

Conflict or Dialogue

It is no secret that many Catholics today disagree with, at any rate, some aspects of the Church's teaching on sexual morality. What does a Catholic do if his (or her) honest reflections lead down a path which appears to be in conflict with the Church's teaching?

When I cannot make my mind up about something, my husband often says to me, 'You don't have enough information'. The first thing to do is therefore to make sure that one has enough information on the subject. Does the Church actually teach what I *think* it teaches? (For instance, it is a common misconception that the mere fact of being divorced excludes someone from communion. It does not.)

What if, even after I have discovered all I can, I still do not agree with, or find it possible to live by, the Church's teaching on, say, contraception? The short answer is that I must nevertheless try to follow this teaching, even though it is beyond my (present) understanding or capacity to obey it.

I think one can give a longer answer too. The Benedictine Rule for monks is often applied to the lives of lay people today and I think the chapter entitled 'If a Brother Be Commanded to Do the Impossible' can throw light on our problem. This chapter states that in the first instance the brother must try to comply with the 'impossible' command. If he still finds he cannot do it, he is to make representations to his superior. However, if the superior remains firm in his command, the Rule states that the brother 'must realise that this is best for him, and trusting in God's help, out of love obey.'

A commentator on the Rule suggests that a comparable situation can arise for lay people who find some aspect of the Church's teaching, e.g. on sexual morality, 'impossible'. He says that the attitude of Catholics should be to try to understand and agree with the teaching, while at the same time seeking sound advice and information. He goes on to say,

> Sometimes the decision [of the Church] can be interpreted more benignly than other none too subtle minds will allow. Still, the first response, the underlying desire, should be to listen to the guidance of the Church, itself guided by the Holy Spirit.[22]

Indeed, the fundamental desire should be to seek, and find, the truth.[23]

St Augustine Again

To return to the question of the morality of sexual pleasure, what are we to say about stances like that of St Augustine? Has his negative view of sex not blocked the full development of the theology of marriage for many centuries? That might appear to be the case, but while he had certainly failed to see something positive, he was also barring the way to a view that the sexual act might be engaged in for sexual pleasure *only*. As I see it, this very 'deficiency' left the path open for the development, at the right time, of a theology of the act of love, which placed not pleasure, but the beloved Other at the centre of the act. In this way Augustine's incomplete understanding of the act of love left room for a fuller understanding in later centuries and particularly in our own.

Conclusion: The New Theology of the Body

The fuller understanding of the gift of self is expressed most poignantly in the teaching of Pope John Paul II which stresses again and again that the mutual gift of the body expresses a total gift of the person.[24] Indeed the dignity and balance of every relationship between a man and a woman depend

> at every moment of history and at every point of geographical longitude and latitude, on *who she will be for him, and he for her*.[25]

By lighting up more fully the picture of the mutual physical gift, Pope John Paul has also shown the way to a healing of the fragmentation of the gift in contemporary society.

In their state of original innocence the first man and woman, Adam and Eve, became a mutual gift for each other and their nakedness emphasised this gift as being from man to woman and woman to man. In the words of Pope John Paul:

> The giving and the accepting of the gift interpenetrate, so that the giving itself becomes accepting, and acceptance is transformed into giving.[26]

This is the marriage relationship as it was originally meant to be, but the late Pope is also holding up an image of what, after Christ, it can be again, and what it surely is in the experience of many a husband and wife. It is no longer possible to return to the state before the Fall, but it is possible to recover the full meaning of the gift, by patiently letting God do his work in us. When this happens, both the fragmentation of the gift in contemporary society and the incomplete view of the gift still found in some church circles are healed and made whole. Against this background, we can now begin to consider the full meaning of the sexual act in marriage.

Summary

Fragmentation, as used in this book, is the division of what properly belongs together. Clarification throws light on what was obscure before. This chapter shows how the gradual clarification of the Church's teaching on marriage can help put together again the fragments of the mutual gift of self in society today.

Further Reading

John Paul II, *The Theology of the Body*, Pauline Books and Media, Boston 1997, esp. pp. 69-72 and159-168.
The sections referred to deal with man and woman as a gift for each other and purity of heart in relation to the gift of the body.

Pat Lynne OCDS, *Edith Stein Discovered:* A Personal Portrait, Gracewing, Leominster (UK), 2000.
The book describes a life lived in search for and obedience to the truth and therefore as an example to everyone seeking to live by the truth.

John Henry Newman, *An Essay on the Development of Christian Doctrine* (First Published 1846), University of Notre Dame Press, Notre Dame, 1990.
A classic work on development in the Christian faith.

See also **Further Reading** for chapter one.

Notes

1 Is 26:1–2 as quoted in Lk 4:18.
2 Apostolic Constitution *Fidei Depositum*, in *Catechism of the Catholic Church*, Geoffrey Chapman, London 1994, p. 4.
3 'The [marriage vows are] merely the sign of the coming into being of marriage. The coming into being of marriage is distinguished from its consummation, to the extent that without this consummation the marriage is not yet constituted in its full reality.' John Paul II, *The Theology of the Body*, Pauline Books and Media, Boston 1997, p. 355.
4 Both quotations from *Catechism of the Catholic Church*, Geoffrey Chapman, London 1994, § 2362.
5 John Paul II, *The Theology of the Body*, pp. 159-73.
6 From *The City of God* as quoted by Gareth Moore OP in *The Body in Context*, Continuum, London and New York 1992. First published by Continuum 2001, p. 46. My description of Augustine's argument follows that of Moore as above.
7 Gareth Moore OP, in *The Body in Context*, p. 48.
8 Ibid., p. 48, quoting *Summa Theologiae*, 1.98.2 ad 3.
9 Summa Theologiae 2-2.153.2 ad 2. (quoted in Gareth Moore OP, *The Body in Context*, p. 50).
10 St Francis de Sales, *Introduction to the Devout Life*, (tr.) John K. Ryan, Second Edition, Revised, Harper Torchbooks, New York 1966, p. 183.
11 Gn 1.1.
12 See especially chapter six.
13 See chapter one.
14 Vincent of Lerins, *Commonitorium*, 2: R 2168. I have based my explanation on Sebastian Bullough, *Roman Catholicism*, Penguin Books, Harmondsworth 1963, pp. 58-9.
15 *Catechism of the Catholic Church*, § 2037.
16 It is not my intention here to give a complete outline of the Catholic Church's teaching on the *Magisterium*. For a full description see *Catechism of the Catholic Church*, §§ 888-92 and 2032-40.
17 *The Code of Canon Law*, English Translation, Collins Liturgical Publications, London 1983. p. 35, Can. 212 § 3.
18 *Catechism of the Catholic Church*, § 2038.
19 Pat Lynne OCDS, *Edith Stein Discovered*, p. 66.
20 http://www.catholicculture.org/docs/doc_view.cfm?recnun=5078 searching under 'Mit Brennender Sorge + Edith Stein'.

21 Bill Huebsch, *Vatican II in Plain English*, vol. 1, The Council, Thomas More Publishing, Allen, Texas, 1997, p. 123.

22 *Work and Prayer*, The Rule of St Benedict for Lay People, Commentary by Columba Cary-Elwes OSB, translation by Catherine Wybourne OSB, Burns and Oates, Tunbridge Wells 1992, pp. 167–8.

23 See chapter seven and eleven.

24 John Paul II, *The Theology of the Body*, Foreword by John S. Grabowski, p. 20.

25 Ibid., p. 157, my emphasis.

26 Ibid., p. 71.

Part Three:

The Gift of Self of in Marriage

Chapter Five

Sex as a Sign of the Gift of Self in Marriage

The sexual act must take place exclusively within marriage.
Catechism of the Catholic Church, 1994[1]

It's not worth dancing with a woman unless you're going to go to bed with her afterwards.
1960s partygoer[2]

'A marriage takes twenty-four hours', a priest friend of mine once said. I had never thought of it quite like that before and was very much struck by his words. What he meant was that no marriage is complete without the gift of self between bride and bridegroom in the act of love. It is this act which makes their commitment irrevocable. In an instant, he had made clear to me just how important the act of love is for the celebration of the sacrament of matrimony.

It was the same priest who said to me, 'When a young couple come to me for marriage preparation, it frequently turns out that they live at the same address. And they always expect me to be shocked.' 'But I don't see why I should be,' he continued, 'after all, Catholics are part of society and in today's society it is usual for couples to live together before marriage, if they marry at all!'

Yet it is the teaching of the Church that the act of love belongs in marriage only. Why is this doctrine now so widely ignored? It is because this teaching, especially with regard to pre-marital sex, is seen as an unreasonable rule laid down by an institution which is out of touch with the times and which

judges harshly those who do not live by its rules. If we are
talking about a regulation, which has become outdated,
because it is now possible to separate sex and procreation, is
it not time that the Church changed its teaching?

On the other hand, if the act of love means more than most
people now see in it, then the 'no sex before marriage' rule
may say something deeper than it is given credit for and this
'something' may need to be said in a new way. As an illus-
tration, I would like to share some of my own experience of
living this seemingly outdated teaching.

The Meaning of Sex: A Personal Reflection

Not so long ago I had a discussion with my husband about the
meaning of sex. I said that, during our marriage, I had come
to see the act of love as a total gift of me to him and him to
me. Each of us could say, 'This is my body. It is for you.' It
seemed to me that no one could give more to anyone and that,
for me, was the compelling reason why this act should take
place only within the lifelong commitment of marriage. I
added, rashly perhaps, that I thought many people would be
able to understand that, whether Christian or not.

He agreed with my view of the act of love, but then added,
'What you've said pre-supposes that people think about the
meaning of the sexual act. Do they really? When are they ever
encouraged to do so?' 'In today's consumer society,' he said,
'many (most?) people do not see their bodies as an integral
part of themselves, but as an item to be used as they please.'
'So *having sex* is a significant expression,' I thought.

'But,' I said, 'a couple might mark their 'point of commitment' to each other by making love, even without an official
ceremony.' He thought that this would rarely be the case.
'Today's relationships are much more fluid,' he said, 'there is
often no definite point of commitment. Many people simply do
what seems (feels) right at the time without stopping to think of
what it means.'

'Why not?' I wondered. Then it came to me, 'because they
are taking sex in contexts other than marriage so much for

granted that there does not appear to be an issue to think about, or discuss.'

It has not always been so. In the last generation or two there has been a significant shift not only in sexual behaviour, but also in the generally accepted norms for such behaviour. The availability of effective contraception has, of course, facilitated this shift.

Shifts in Sexual morality in the Last Two Generations

There has always been sex outside marriage, but those who were involved in it knew that they were going against the accepted norms and did not broadcast what they were doing. An older friend of mine, who was at university just after the Second World War and who later became a lecturer herself, put it this way, 'In my student days there were a few girls who slept with their boyfriends, but we knew who they were and they weren't the nice ones. Now, with the students I teach, the nice ones do it too.'

The shift she had noticed appears in the statistics too, which show that, in the 1950s, hardly any British couples lived together before marriage, whereas, by the late 1980s, almost half did so.[3] At the time of writing a further shift has taken place, with many couples living together without any intention of getting married.

Examples from Literature

The recent shifts in sexual morality can be seen in literature as well as in life around us.

Nevil Shute: *A Town like Alice*

In his well-known novel, *A Town Like Alice,* which first came out in 1950, Nevil Shute describes the courtship and marriage between a young Australian, Joe, and the English girl, Jean, whom he first meets during the Second World War in Japanese-occupied Malaya.

Their budding romance is interrupted, when they are captured by the Japanese. With his help she manages to escape, but it is only after the war that she learns that he has been tortured for this, surviving only through a quirk of Japanese 'red tape'. Both are left with a longing for the other, which eventually leads them to go in search of each other and to find each other again, six years after they first met. The culmination of this search takes place at a resort in Australia where they have rented two 'beach huts' to have a chance to talk and to get to know each other again.

The social context was still one which assumed that a man and a woman would sleep together only after they were married. However, it was only a few years after a war which had broken many standards that had previously been taken for granted, including that of 'waiting till after we are married'. In wartime there often was no 'after'. So Jean and Joe meet at a time and place when many lived by the accepted standards, while others departed from them. During their few days on the beach they face the kinds of decisions, which any couple who want the act of love to be more than 'something that happened', have to face. It can therefore speak to any couple, any time. In the book, we are allowed to follow Jean's thoughts more than Joe's, but it is obvious that they are both thinking about marriage and wondering whether a marriage between them would work.

It is also clear that, at Joe's suggestion of a few days away together, on the beach, Jean, who has never slept with anyone, wonders whether he is expecting to make love to her, and, because of that, lays down some ground rules. She insists on paying her share of the expenses (and on *two* 'beach huts'!). In other words, she wants to remain free to make her own decisions and he respects this.

We are not told exactly what his expectations are, but Jean certainly thinks she will have to say 'no' a few times during the weekend. She has also taken it for granted that they will reach some sort of 'emotional conclusion' during these few days alone together. Instead nothing at all happens and she feels there is a 'heavy restraint' between them, perhaps because he last saw her as a bloodstained refugee in Malaya, barefoot, and wearing a sarong. Now she is a beautiful English girl in a frock and with money too.

If Joe had not gone all the way to England to look for her (while she was looking for him in Australia), she would not have believed that he really cared for her at all. She goes on to reflect that, if Joe had been so interested in an Australian girl from Cairns, they would have been in bed by now. (Is Jean slightly prejudiced about the sexual morality of Australians?). At any rate Jean thinks that *something* should have happened and she would certainly have liked to be kissed under the stars!

She decides that it is worth taking a bit of a risk for Joe and changes into a sarong very like the one she had worn when they last met, six years ago. She comes to him rather shyly, asking 'Is this better, Joe?' and it is so much 'better' that

> in the tumult of feelings that swept over her she knew that this man wanted her as nobody had ever wanted her before.

In her confusion she says that they can be seen from the house nearby.

> The next thing that she realised was that they were in her bedroom hut ... And now a new confusion came over her ... She could feel her [sarong] ... getting loose and falling, and she had no other garment on at all.

In situations like this we would so much like time to think, but life is not always like that, as Jean now discovers:

> Standing in his arms still unresisting, smothered by his kisses, she thought, this is It. And then she thought, It had to happen sometime, and I'm glad it's Joe. And then she thought, It's not his fault, I brought this on myself. And then she thought, I must sit down or something, or I'll be stark-naked, and at that she escaped backwards from his arms and sat down on the bed.

In her innocence and inexperience Jean has not reckoned with the full effect that the sight and sensation of her in the sarong

will have on Joe, nor has she thought about the sheer prac-
ticalities of a sarong standing up to 'energetic man-handling'.

> He followed her down, laughing, and her eyes laughed back at
> him as she tried to hold her sarong up with her hand to hide her
> bosom. Then she was in his arms again and he was hindering
> her. And then he said quite simply, 'Do you mind?'

He is by now overcome by his feelings for her, but not to such
an extent that he forgets to ask her what *she* wants and his
question makes Jean aware of what she most deeply wants.
Her thoughts have moved from 'this is It' to 'I'm glad it's
Joe,' to 'It's not his fault, I brought this on myself.' So, when
he asks, 'Do you mind?', her reply continues her train of
thought, 'Not if you've got to.' (She is thinking of how much
he has already suffered for her). 'If you can wait till we're
married, I'd much rather ...'

She says this so lovingly that it can in no way be interpreted
as a rejection of *him*. 'Will you marry me?', he says ... 'Of
course I'll marry you ... What do you think I came to
Australia for?'

Realising the depth of her love and commitment, Joe recov-
ers himself,

> He grinned; he was holding her more gently now. 'I don't know
> what you must think of me.'
> 'Shall I tell you?' She took one of his wounded hands in hers
> and fondled the great scars. 'I think you're the man I want to
> marry and have children by.' ... 'I'd rather wait a few months
> and get our lives arranged a little first, Joe. Marriage is a big
> thing, and there are things that ought to be done, first, before
> we marry. But if you say we can't wait, then I'll marry you
> tomorrow, or tonight.'
> He drew her to him gently, and kissed her fingertips. 'I can
> wait. I've waited six years for this, and I can wait a bit longer.'

And later,

> I can wait a long time for you, after this.[4]

I have quoted this passage at some length, because it shows so much of what can happen between a man and a woman who are deeply in love. Jean's decision that she would much rather wait till they are married before making love would be rare in our times, but the respect that both Joe and Jean show for each other's thoughts and feelings belongs in every loving relationship.

Rosamunde Pilcher: *The Shell Seekers*

Joe and Jean belong to roughly the same generation as the older friend I mentioned earlier, but she and her contemporaries were just young enough not to have been directly involved in the war and therefore might have accepted the pre-war attitude to sexual morality in a more unquestioning way.

A novel, which came out some thirty years after *Alice*, shows very different attitudes to sex. In *The Shell Seekers* Rosamunde Pilcher describes the developing relationship between a young man and a woman in very different terms. The couple reach a stage where they each feel that the other is part of their lives, at which point they begin to sleep together. Marriage is 'in the air' but not a certainty.

In Pilcher's book, written a generation after *Alice*, there is no indication of any agonising on their part about the rightness or wrongness of what they are doing. They simply do what appears to be the natural next step in their relationship, but the girl shows her awareness of shifting standards between generations, when, during a car journey, she makes it clear to a much-loved aunt that she and the young man have slept together.

[The girl's] charming profile was intent on the road ahead, but a faint blush warmed her cheeks.
[The aunt] turned back to look out of the window, smiling secretly to herself. She said, 'I *am* glad'.[5]

Interestingly, there is a passing reference to the young couple going to church, later in the book. Does the aunt's reaction reflect the author's own attitude? Is she trying to say that sleeping together before marriage is compatible with Christian belief or, at any rate with the beliefs, of some Christians?[6]

Libby Purves: *Holy Smoke*

Describing her own attitude to sex as a young Catholic woman in the late 1960s, the British author and broadcaster Libby Purves says that she was not married then and stayed a long time chaste.[7]

There is a striking contrast between Purves' own life as a young woman and what she describes, in middle age, as acceptable behaviour by young people in their late teens. In *Nature's Masterpiece, A Family Survival Book*, published in the year 2000, she says, addressing the parent generation, that,

> 'If you disapprove of bed-sharing outside marriage you do not have to condone it. On the other hand, in the case of a pair a committed seventeen-year-olds, you may decide to do just that rather than have them take risks elsewhere.'[8]

Her assumption is that, at the beginning of the Second Millennium, there is a range of choices about sexual behaviour, several of which are morally defensible.

It should be added that there are reasons other than moral ones affecting a couple's choice to live together or not. For couples a bit older than those envisaged by Libby Purves, economic and practical considerations can play an important part in such a decision. A couple sharing can live much more cheaply than two people in individual accommodation. If money is tight, and the two of them want to be together, for the time being anyway, why not live at the same address and save money? It takes a strong and well-informed conviction that sex belongs exclusively in marriage to make a couple resist the temptation presented by this argument.

Helen Fielding: *Bridget Jones's Diary*

In *Bridget Jones's Diary*, a slightly facetious novel about the life and sexual *mores* of 'Millennium Woman', the author, Helen Fielding, has the heroine say, after she has been to bed with the man of her dreams,

> Oh joy. Have spent the day . . . mooning about the flat, smiling, picking things up and putting them down again . . .
>
> But as the rosy clouds begin to disperse, I begin to feel alarm. What now? No plans were made. Suddenly I realise that I am waiting for the phone again . . .
>
> Oh God. Why hasn't Daniel rung? Are we going out now, or what?[9]

This book is roughly contemporary with *Nature's Masterpiece*, but it has moved one step further in the direction of uncertainty about sexual behaviour. Libby Purves speaks of sex as acceptable in a *committed* relationship outside marriage. Helen Fielding sees her heroine as totally uncertain about the meaning of the sexual act. Admittedly, it is described as an expression of (uncertain) love towards the end of the book,[10] but we are a long way from the world of principles and informed choices about sex, which the previous works inhabit. On the other hand, the popularity of *Bridget Jones* indicates that it strikes a chord with many a woman (and man?) today. Indeed, one cannot help feeling for Bridget in what is, in spite of appearances, a genuine search for love.

My Experience

Being of roughly the same generation as Libby Purves, I too was brought up to believe that sex belonged in marriage and nowhere else. There was certainly an assumption that no 'good Catholic' would engage in sexual relations outside marriage. Behind all this there was, also, the unspoken fear of a child outside wedlock and the Victorian *eleventh command-*

ment 'thou shalt not be found out' was not far away.

My friends and I accepted the 'no sex outside marriage' rule often, I suspect, without thinking very deeply about the reasons for this prohibition, especially as far as sex *before* marriage was concerned. If asked at the time, I might have said that I wanted to give myself to my husband 'untouched' and that, once we were married, making love would be a wonderful way of showing, fully, what we felt for each other.

It was only later that, through the experience of married life, I came to understand that the gift of my body meant the gift of *me*. I now realise that it is not enough to say about sex outside marriage, 'It is not done', even if the rule was short-hand for something deeper. It is necessary to point to the meaning of the sexual act as a total and lifelong gift of self between a man and a woman, which can therefore only be given with its full significance within marriage.

When a prominent British politician in the 1990s chose to share a bedroom with his fiancée at the party conference, it was commented on in the press as an official abandonment of the pretence that couples did not live together before marriage. In this 'official' acceptance of sex outside marriage, which is linked to the fragmentation of the sexual act mentioned in the previous chapter, our age is radically different from previous ages, even those within a generation or two of our own.

The Teaching of the Church in a New Context

In spite of the social climate now, the Church still teaches that sex belongs in marriage only, even though few people live like that. Living one's faith as a Catholic today means, as the Bishops' Conference of England and Wales has put it, being 'unlike most of our contemporaries'.[11] The current situation is therefore an invitation to reflect more deeply on the teaching of the Church in this area and to ask, 'What does the physical gift of self in marriage mean?'

The Act of Love within the Sacrament of Matrimony

'A Marriage takes twenty-four hours', my priest friend had said, thus highlighting the importance of the act of love within the sacrament of matrimony. His words made it clear that sex is not just 'something nice' that one is allowed to do, once married, or a kind of reward for patient waiting! With this in mind, let us look at the Roman Catholic marriage service, which, in the eyes of the Church, marks the beginning of the lifelong gift of self of bride and groom to each other.

The celebration of the sacrament of matrimony in the Catholic Church begins with the exchange of vows by the couple in the presence of witnesses. Normally a priest or deacon receives the consent of the parties to the marriage on behalf of the Church, but the ministers of the sacrament (the visible sign of an inner transformation) are the bride and groom themselves.[12]

Their will to 'establish a partnership of the whole of life'[13] is the foundation of the marriage, but Christ underpins their awesome commitment with his gift of grace, so that they can be faithful to each other, as he is to the Church.

The bride and groom take each other to be

My wedded wife – my wedded husband – to have, and to hold from this day forward, for better for worse ... till death do us part ...[14]

The gift of the body is implied in the words 'to have and to hold', which are spoken by both bride and groom individually. In the old rite, the physical gift also found powerful expression in the words that were spoken by the groom only, but which surely apply equally to bride and groom,

... with my body I thee worship ...[15]

The commitment of the couple to each other is total, made with all their love, all their will and all their strength, but it is also a commitment 'in the Lord', as the words spoken by the priest after the marriage vows make clear:

You have declared your consent before the Church. May the
Lord in his goodness *strengthen* your consent [through the grace
of the sacrament] and fill you both with his blessings.

What God has joined together, let no man put asunder.[16]

After the marriage liturgy, family and friends gather for a
celebration meal and all the festivities that go with a wedding.
But 'the marriage is not yet constituted in its full
reality'.[17]After leaving the celebration, when they are alone
together, the bride and groom, the two ministers of the sacrament, give themselves to each other in the act of love.

This is the consummation, the 'becoming flesh', without
which the wedding promises would remain unfulfilled.[18] It is
a gift of the whole person, body, soul and spirit, which sets
the seal on the marriage vows and makes them irrevocable.

Living the Gift

The act of love is only the first of many such acts through
which the couple will grow in love. The philosopher Dietrich
von Hildebrand, himself a married man, put it beautifully
when he said that a couple can only make love in the right way
when they can do so 'in the sight of God'.[19] Married couples
are invited to give themselves to each other in the act of love,
so that, with each gift of self, they grow closer to each other
and to the Lord. After many years of marriage I know that the
full meaning of the act unfolds gradually and indeed that it can
only realise its potential within the trusting commitment of a
lifelong gift.

The Gift in Our Times

I have described the celebration of the sacrament of matrimony and the place of the act of love within it as it was meant
to be 'from the beginning'.[20] However, in our times, there are
many people who have had intercourse long before marriage,
without understanding the full significance of the act of love.

Since most couples who come for marriage preparation live together, it follows that only a tiny minority approach their wedding in the state of virginity assumed by, or at any rate much wished for, by the Church.

So what happens when a man and a woman who are living together or have had previous sexual relationships, begin to realise the full significance of the act of love? Surely, there must be a way back? Yes, there is, because this realisation is also, *always*, a chance to put the past behind them and begin again and I will return to this question later in this chapter and in chapter twelve. But first I want to consider the mutual attraction, which sets the 'scene' for the act of love.

Attraction and the Gift of Self

The word 'attraction' means being drawn towards someone or something. The attraction between a man and a woman usually has a strong physical aspect, indeed, this kind of attraction can be experienced as so powerful that it seems to the two people as if they have no choice but to yield to it; but can that be true?

Freedom and Responsibility

A priest, whose wisdom I had grown to respect, once said to me, 'I think the furthest one can get in one's development as a person is to know, fully, one's motivation for any particular action.' He did not say, but I think it follows, that someone who knows their motivation also has the opportunity to influence their actions at source. Clearly, this is not how we begin in life and there can be few people who cannot echo St Paul's words about doing what he did not want to do and not doing what he did want to do.[21] We grow into responsibility for our actions and this takes time.

Our freedom, and hence our responsibility, is sometimes impaired by the influence of our surroundings and that is particularly true in matters of sexual behaviour. If the spoken or unspoken assumption in society or in my circle of friends is that it is 'only natural', as one friend put it, 'to sleep with one's boy or girlfriend', then it takes enormous courage and independence of spirit not to do so.

When my husband and I decided to stick to the principles we had been brought up with by not living together before marriage, there was still a generally accepted moral framework to support this. In that sense our choice was not as difficult as it would have been now, when even many Christians think it is all right for engaged couples to sleep together. In today's society the choice to live by the teaching of the Catholic Church, and that of other Christian churches, is a lonely one.

When Attraction Overwhelms

When we were engaged, my husband once said, 'If we had started sleeping together, I hope it would have been because we had decided that that was the right thing to do, not because it had just happened.' In other words, he thought that something as important as this should be decided before the situation arose.

A friend of mine once told me that, there were times during her engagement, when her fiancé hardly dared touch her, because they both so very much wanted to make love and were finding the time of waiting hard. I can remember a similar experience during my own engagement, when we both had to 'stand back', so that we could stick to our decision to make love only after we were married. Yet attraction can overwhelm and only God knows how free any particular man or woman was at the time.

Special Cases

In some cases the physical loss of virginity is outside a person's control, in others, the man or woman may have had only minimal, if any, responsibility for what happened. It goes without saying that, in cases of rape and other sex abuse, there is no fundamental loss of virginity or chastity on the part of the victim, no matter how he or she may feel about what has been done to them.

It is also worth mentioning the general effect that low self-esteem (often the result of some form of abuse) can have on a man or a woman. The physical gift of oneself to another person presupposes that the giver considers the gift worth giving and therefore also worth receiving. It presupposes a proper love of self, because I cannot love others as myself, unless I love myself in the first place!

The problem with low self-esteem is precisely that the person concerned considers him or her self of low value, and therefore unlovable. A man or woman in this predicament may make, or accept, sexual advances, simply because it makes them feel desirable. The act of sex boosts their damaged image of self, so that it is not the wish to give themselves to another that motivates their action, but the desperate need to be considered of value, by someone.

People who have found themselves acting in this way need healing, not condemnation and the Catechism of the Catholic Church acknowledges this when it says that

> R esponsibility for an action can be diminished or even nullified by ignorance, inadvertence, duress, fear, habit, *inordinate attachments* and other *psychological* or social factors.[22]

Justice and Mercy

The Woman Caught in Adultery

Many people believe that the Church and 'good' Christians are particularly judgemental in matters of sexual transgression. Though there may be some truth in that, one has only to turn to the Gospels to discover the very different example set by Christ himself in such matters. The account of the woman caught in adultery is revealing about attitudes to sexual sin.

Jesus is teaching in the Temple, when some of the Pharisees bring along a woman who has been caught 'in the very act of committing adultery', as they say.[23] According to the Law of

Moses she should be stoned. The Bible does not say this explicitly, but one can imagine the Pharisees, full of (self) righteous indignation, saying, 'Of course she should be stoned!' Jesus says nothing, but simply looks at the ground.

Eventually, when pressed, he says, 'Let the one among you who is guiltless be the first to throw a stone at her.' They all fade away, beginning with the eldest, and Jesus is left alone with the woman.

The interaction between the two is illuminating. Jesus treats her with infinite courtesy and tact and while the men are still there, he does not even look at her, but writes in the sand. Only after they have left does he look up and speak to her, not to admonish her, but to seek information from her. In other words, he treats her as an equal,

> 'Woman, where are they? Has no one condemned you?' 'No one, sir' she replied. 'Neither do I condemn you ... go away and from this moment sin no more.'[24]

Jesus treats her with both mercy ('Neither do I condemn you') and justice ('sin no more'). What the woman has done is wrong in itself, but that is not where Jesus begins. He shows her mercy and consideration first. He welcomes her and makes it clear that he values her opinion. In fact, he may be the first man ever to treat her with respect. In doing so he begins to build up her self-esteem and takes away what may well have been the reason for her adultery. (*Someone* had found her desirable, at least for a moment.) By treating her as someone truly of value Jesus sets her free. His next words, therefore, do not come as a condemnation, but as an invitation to leave her sin behind, now that she is free to do so.

In this exchange between Jesus and the woman, mercy, which empathises with her situation, and justice, which shows her the truth about it, come together and open up a new path of freedom and responsibility, for her, and for all who ponder this text.

The Men

But, one might ask, what about the men in the story? Since the woman had been caught in adultery, there must, of necessity, have been a man caught with her! We hear nothing about the man and can only assume that those who caught them judged her much more harshly than him, and let him escape. It is interesting that the Law of Moses in fact judges the man and the woman equally harshly, saying that, if caught in adultery, both should be put to death, but the men of our story have conveniently forgotten about that.[25]

Nevertheless, these men were not totally insensitive to male sexual sin. At Jesus' invitation to the one without sin to throw the first stone, they all slink away, beginning with the eldest. They may not all have committed sexual sin, but one cannot help thinking that one or two of them suddenly saw a similar scene in their minds' eye, and recognised themselves in the face of the man. Perhaps, for these, it was the beginning of a change of heart.

The Prodigal Son

In order to find a Gospel account of a man who was certainly converted from a life of sexual sin, we have to turn to the well-known story of the Prodigal Son. A man has two sons, the younger of whom asks for his share of the inheritance, which he then squanders on 'a life of debauchery'.[26] When he has used up all his money, and is starving, he comes to his senses and repents.

The return of the Prodigal Son and the merciful and generous forgiveness of his father have been depicted in numerous works of art. The reaction of the elder brother who had stayed at home is perhaps less well-known. This brother feels that he is being treated unfairly, because the father has put on a great party to celebrate the return of the younger son. The elder brother is furious, feeling that he should be the one to be fêted, since he has never broken any of the commandments. He is particularly scathing about the sexual aspect of the younger brother's misdemeanours, 'he and his loose women'.[27]

The behaviour of the elder brother in this story is very like that of the Pharisees in 'The Adulterous Woman'. He does not think that he has anything to repent of at all, whereas the younger brother, who is totally repentant ('I no longer deserve to be called your son'[28]), can leave all his sins behind, including the sexual ones. In the Father's words to the elder son:

> It is only right we should celebrate and rejoice, because your brother here was dead and has come to life; he was lost and is found.[29]

The emphasis in this account is not as specifically focused on sexual sin as in the tale of the adulterous woman, but here, too, truthfulness ('he was lost') is paired with merciful forgiveness ('he is found – let us celebrate'). Sin has been left behind.

The Way Back

In Jewish society at the time of Jesus there were definite rules about sexual morality, but in our society today, the situation is less clear. No doubt most people would still consider adultery as seriously harmful to marriage, but there are many other cases of sexual intercourse outside marriage, which were until recently considered equally wrong, such as premarital sex or living together without being married. Many of these are now thought to be perfectly acceptable, at any rate those that occur in a committed relationship.

'I Did not Know'

Someone wanting to lead a Christian life in our times is, in many ways, in a similar situation to the early converts to Christianity. He or she will not be persecuted, but their way of life will become significantly different to that of most people around them. In terms of sexual morality, it is probable that the convert, or the Christian who begins to take a closer look at his or her lifestyle, will already have had one or more sexual partners before or outside marriage. Many such people have acted in good faith, or, at any rate, with a minimal awareness of the full meaning of the act of love. How is somebody in this situation to return to a way of life that is compatible with the teaching of Christ? Jesus' words to the woman caught in adultery and others in comparable situations make it abundantly clear that anyone can be set free from such a background.

At the time of writing the decision of a number of American teenagers to commit themselves to sexual abstinence before marriage has been widely reported in the press. The *Silver Ring Thing*, one of a number of American programmes advocating sexual abstinence before marriage, is now also being introduced into the UK. A British programme called *Oasis Esteem* is run in a number of schools and has been described as helpful in making teenagers think for themselves.[30]

The immediate intention of these programmes was a reduction in the increasingly high incidence of sexually transmitted infections among young people, but most are inspired by Evangelical Christianity and also advocate sexual abstinence before marriage as an important aspect of Christian living. There is evidence that the American programme is beginning to show results in terms of disease reduction and although about 90% of teenagers who have pledged themselves to remain virgin till marriage, break their promise, the 10%, who do not, form a much larger percentage of the group than the figures quoted for the British population at large.[31] Some of these programmes are used in Catholic schools in the context of Catholic teaching on sexual morality.[32]

The programmes stress the importance of giving people a 'second chance', so that it is always possible to begin from where you are. In other words, understanding the full meaning of the sexual act must not lead to a sad 'If only', but rather to a trusting 'Now I can'.[33]

In the final analysis, it is the spirit that forms the body and not the body that shapes the spirit. Having sex outside marriage is a fragmented action, but the healing of this fragmentation can lead to a 'virginity regained', with all the promise of a new beginning. Speaking of this spiritual virginity, chosen later in life, Pope John Paul II said, with both realism and compassion,

> We must remember that human life can be and should be a quest for a road to God, an ever better and ever shorter road.[34]

He was referring mainly to those with a call to the religious life, but I think his words apply with equal force to people with a vocation to marriage.

The Harder Path

Not so long ago I listened to an interview with the abbot of an enclosed monastery. When asked about the background from which his novices came and how they managed to live a celibate life, he said, 'Nowadays, they have nearly always been in (sexual) relationships and it takes two to three years for the effects of this to be healed.' Deciding to become 'spiritually virgin', whether it is in order to respond to a religious or priestly vocation, or, more commonly, to give oneself in marriage, means treading a hard path.

A friend of mine, who had been seeing her future husband, on and off, for several years, until the relationship finally resolved itself and they married, once said to me, 'Of course, if either of us had lived with someone before we met, we could not have waited all that time before making love.' I do not think that I agree with her, but I am sure that it must be much more difficult to 'wait', if one has at some stage in one's life 'not waited'.

Remaining virgin until marriage or, for those who do not marry, for life, is what I would wish for everyone and what the Church asks of all of us. However, in our times, it is only realistic to assume that for most couples the path to a complete gift of self in marriage goes through a return to chastity, and hence spiritual virginity, before marriage.

How can this be done? I would not presume to make

suggestions, because here each couple must find the path that is right for them. All I can do is to point to my own much lesser difficulty during my engagement and say, 'Love grows at such a time.'

Sex as a Gift of Self in Marriage in Our Times

When a couple marry, they give themselves to each other, for life. They express their gift in the words of the marriage vows and seal it by giving themselves in the act of love. The gift of the body is so highly valued by Christ and the Church that it is used as an image of Christ's gift of himself to the Church and of his total faithfulness.

Society in general also considers sex important, but for different reasons. 'Having sex', in the sense of 'enjoying the pleasure of sex', is often regarded as a right and is not infrequently detached from any commitment, as the passage from *Bridget Jones* has illustrated. Against this background great respect is due to any man or woman who wants to give the act its full value, wherever life may have taken them on the way to that decision.

Summary

This chapter considers the significance of the act of love in relation to the sacrament of matrimony. It looks at attraction, freedom and responsibility in relation to this act. It also considers sexual intercourse outside marriage and the meaning of virginity in the context of behavioural patterns today and in the recent past.

Further Reading

John Paul II, *The Theology of the Body*: *Human Love in the Divine Plane*, Pauline Books and Media, Boston 1997, especially pp. 354–7.

Karol Wojtyla [John Paul II] *Love and Responsibility*, Collins

Fount Paperbacks, London 1982, translated from Polish by H.
T. Willetts. Also published by Ignatius Press, San Francisco
1994.
A demanding, but highly rewarding book.

*The Complete Rite of Marriage, with Nuptial Mass, for the use
. . . of dioceses of England and Wales*, Catholic Truth Society,
London 1976.

See also **Further Reading** for chapter six.

Notes
 1 *Catechism of the Catholic Church*, Geoffrey Chapman, London
   1994, § 2390.
 2 Comment as reported to author.
 3 *Population Trends*, Summer 1999, Office of National Statistics,
   London.
 4 Nevil Shute, *A Town Like Alice*, First published by William
   Heineman Ltd, 1950. Quotations in this book refer to the edition
   published by House of Stratus, London, 2000, pp. 251-3.
 5 Rosamunde Pilcher, *The Shell Seekers*, New English Library,
   Sevenoaks, 1987, reprinted 1988, p. 435.
 6 Ibid., p. 502.
 7 Libby Purves, *Holy Smoke, Religion and Roots: A Personal
   Memoir*, Hodder & Stoughton, London, Sydney, Auckland,
   1998, p. 138.
 8 Libby Purves, *Nature's Masterpiece, A Family Survival Book*,
   Hodder and Stoughton, London 2000, p. 199f.
 9 Helen Fielding, *Bridget Jones's Diary*, Picador, London 1996,
   p. 60.
10 Ibid., p. 306f.
11 'On the Threshold', the Report of the Bishops' Conference
   Working Party on Sacramental Initiation, published on behalf of
   the Bishops' Conference of England and Wales by Matthew
   James Publishing Ltd, 19 Wellington Close, Chelmsford Essex
   CM1 2EE, 2000, p. 25.
12 In the traditions of the Eastern churches, 'the priests (bishops or
   presbyters) are witnesses to the mutual consent given by the
   spouses, but for the validity of the sacrament their blessing is also
   necessary.' *Catechism of the Catholic Church*, § 1623, as amended

in *Briefing*, 18 September 1997, vol. 27, Issue 9, p. 30.

13 *Catechism of the Catholic Church* § 1601.

14 *The Complete Rite of Marriage with Nuptial Mass*, Catholic Truth Society, London 1976, p. 34.

15 *The Marriage Service and Nuptial Rite*, Catholic Truth Society, London 1968, p. 5.

16 *The Complete Rite of Marriage with Nuptial Mass*, p. 35. My italics.

17 John Paul II, *The Theology of the Body*, p. 355f.

18 That is why a marriage which has not been consummated can be dissolved.

19 Dietrich von Hildebrand, *In Defence of Purity*, Sheed and Ward, London 1931, p. 27.

20 Mk 10:6.

21 Rm 7:19. It is rewarding to read the whole context of Rm 7:14-20.

22 *Catechism of the Catholic Church*, § 1735. My emphasis.

23 Jn 8:5.

24 Jn 8:10-11.

25 Dt 22:22.

26 Lk 15:13.

27 Ibid., 15:30.

28 Ibid., 15:21.

29 Ibid., 15:32.

30 Trevor Stammers 'Taking the Pledge' in *The Tablet*, 29 May 2004 and Karen Robinson 'School for Sex' in *The Sunday Times*, 16 May 2004.

31 See chapter one.

32 See for instance, Caryle Murphy, 'Programs Help Teens Sort Out Sex, Morality Issues', in Washington Post, Sunday, 6 April 2003, which refers to the Catholic Archdiocese of Washington and Diocese of Hereford News, 5 March 2004, which refers to use of the 'Challenge' programme in a Catholic school in the area, (http://www.hereford.anglican.org/pages/news_pressrelease.php ?Challeng-Team.txt).

33 See especially Patrick Barkham 'Teens told a Silver Ring and a Vow of Chastity Are the Best Way to Combat Sexual Epidemic', in *The Guardian*, 10 May 2004.

34 Karol Wojtyla [John Paul II] *Love and Responsibility*, p. 253.

Chapter Six

The Holy of Holies

My love is mine and I am his.
Song of Songs 2:16

By means of the body, the human person is husband and wife.
Pope John Paul II[1]

The expression 'the Holy of Holies' is used about the most holy, the most special place anywhere. This is where we reach the centre, the most hidden secret of a person or a religion. The Holy of Holies can be different things to different people. Children sometimes have 'secret places' that are theirs alone and where no one else is allowed to come. To a writer, the 'Holy of Holies' might be the place where he or she writes and where other people enter only by invitation.

Religions, too, have their 'Holy of Holies'. During the Old Testament period only the High Priest was allowed to enter the 'Holy of Holies' in the Temple, and that only once a year.[2] The Holy of Holies does not have to be a place, it can be a diary, for instance, where someone reveals their most secret thoughts, for no one's eyes but their own. Revealing my secret thoughts in speech to another person means, in a very real sense, that I am letting him or her into my Holy of Holies.

Revealing Myself in the Act of Love

Revealing my body to another person in the act of love also means letting them enter the Holy of Holies, not only of my body, but of my whole self. Indeed, through the act of love husband and wife enter into the sanctuary of their marriage. The fact that many couples will have experienced sex before marriage, with each other, or with other people, does not mean that they cannot give the gift its full meaning, once they know what that meaning is. Indeed, whether or not the spouses have experienced sex before marriage, it is likely that one or both will have to learn to trust someone of the opposite sex again after experiences of disappointment and rejection. In this way the expression of their love for each other will also become an act of healing.[3]

The Wrong Eyes

Because letting someone else into my most secret place, whether of body of mind, is an act of complete trust, rejection by the 'other' is a crushing blow.

In his book *The Loop* Nicholas Evans describes the reaction of a woman, Helen, in just this situation. She has let Joel into her life, has given him her body, has told him all she felt there was to tell him about herself. She thought that he, too, had given himself to her in this way, though a permanent commitment had never been spoken of. When he begins to withdraw from the relationship, she is all but destroyed, because she knows that

> This time she had not just sought to please but had opened every corner of herself. There was no part of her he didn't know, nothing with which she could console herself and say, had he but seen this in me, then surely he never would or could have gone. She had given all and still been found wanting.[4]

When Joel finally leaves her for another woman, Helen attempts suicide. Her reaction is understandable. She takes his rejection to what, to her, seems the inevitable conclusion.

The Whole Person

What struck me about Helen and Joel's relationship was the fact that, for her at least, the gift of self was total, body, mind, everything. In her subconscious she had begun to assume that the gift would be permanent, which reveals something about the nature of the gift: It is meant for permanence. When I fragment it by 'having sex' without any intention of a permanent relationship, then I cause terrible damage both to myself and the other person.

What is more, the potential for physical union is not an 'added extra' but a God-given, integral part of what it means to be human. Adrienne von Speyr, a mid-twentieth century Swiss medical doctor and theological writer, put it beautifully when she said,

> Man and woman together are created in the image and likeness of God, and the image of God has its seat not in a soul thought of as sexless but in the whole human person, who is a unified being consisting of body and spirit.[5]

One could add that we now know that the chromosomes of every cell of a human being shows the sex of that person. The human person, as man or woman, is indeed 'a unified being' and the gift of the human being is a unified gift.

My Body – Freely Given

It is the gift of my whole self, me as a 'unified being' that takes place in the act of love between husband and wife. This gift implies a profound reverence for the other person, who is giving himself or herself to me. The sense of awe before the other person was expressed in the old marriage rite in the words 'with my body I thee worship'.[6] To 'worship' means to give value to' or to consider 'of worth'. In the act of love husband and wife show each other how much they value, respect and indeed revere each other.

It is therefore not surprising that the word worship is also, and now mainly, used about our relationship with God. The two kinds of love are not the same, but the fact that the same word has come to be used about both shows that love is linked with a sense of reverence for the beloved. It is with this sense of awe that the bride and groom give themselves in the act of love, thus making their spoken promises incarnate.

Self-Revelation and Closeness

'All deep love seeks union', a friend once said to me, and union is only possible through mutual self revelation. I need to know the person I love and be known by him or her.

In married love this self-revelation is taken as far as it is possible between human beings in the mutual gift of self that is the act of love. Being close to someone means being physically as well as spiritually close to him or her. An intimate conversation is not shouted across a room, love does not seem (is not!) real, until it has been given a physical expression. But this expression does not come automatically. The whole of the act of love has rightly been described as a language. How can a couple know, before they marry, that they will be able to speak it with each other?

The Question of Compatibility

When I discussed this chapter with a friend, she said, echoing the view of many people, 'It's all very well saying that the act of love belongs in marriage only, but how do you know that you will be sexually compatible? Once you are married, it's too late to discover that you aren't!'

In her novel *Casting Off*, set in post-Second World War England, Elizabeth Jane Howard tells the story of a middle-aged couple, Hugh and Jemima, both widowed, who confront this problem by going to bed, just once, before they marry:

> He had asked her whether she wanted to go to bed with him before marrying, had said that it should be her choice ... And so, because she had had lingering fears ... was afraid that she would disappoint either herself or him – she had agreed.

She discovers that he is the perfect lover for her,

... patient, sensitive, delightful and full of ardour.

According to the novel, both now feel reassured that the marriage will be a success in every respect.[7] Maybe some people do discover sexual harmony at the first attempt, and, of course, this couple is not making love for the first time in their lives. Even so, I am not convinced that what happens between Hugh and Jemima is typical.

Whenever I read a description of a couple going to bed for the first time and am told that it was 'wonderful', I am reminded of the words of another friend, who said, 'This business of sex being wonderful the first time is largely fiction, I think. It must be so much easier to write, "and they went to bed and it was fantastic" than to say, "actually, it took time to learn".'

This learning process naturally begins before the couple marry, so that, even without sleeping together, they will know something about how they each react sexually. I think it is very important to talk about this, in openness and mutual trust, before the marriage takes place.

There is a German proverb which roughly translates as 'One can't have a trial life, a trial love, or a trial death'.[8] We only live once and we only die once. There is no such thing as a 'practice run' for life. Similarly, there is no such thing as a 'practice run' for loving somebody and there is certainly no 'practice run' for giving oneself in the act of love, which seals a marriage. The gift is a sign, not of sexual compatibility, but, as the Church teaches, of a total gift of the person, and there can be no 'trial run' for that.[9]

Sometimes people who are not married can throw interesting light on what marriage is like. A celibate friend of mine once said, rather diffidently, 'You know, in our civilisation, competence sometimes seems to be all. *Quick – instant – perfect* seems to be the order of the day, in sexual matters too. So many people think that if sex is not instantly wonderful, there must be something wrong with the relationship.'

'Surely that can't be so,' he went on. 'Couples learn to be together in all sorts of ways, it's all part of growing together. Patience, joy, discovery – and humour must all come into it,' he said, 'don't they?' I could only marvel at his perception. I think it can be helpful to draw a parallel with learning a new language. To begin with, I am likely to be more concerned with grammar and vocabulary than with what I am actually saying, but once I have mastered the language, I can concentrate more fully on what I want to say. In the same way, it has been my experience that there is a shift in emphasis, in a marriage, from the physical actions in lovemaking to the deepening love that they express. Since arousal normally occurs much more quickly in a man than a woman, the way in which our bodies have been created itself invites patience and an ever-growing mutual understanding.[10]

The Song of Songs: *Sexual Desire in God's Revelation*

The delight of the physical gift of self is beautifully described in the Old Testament Book The Song of Songs, a collection of Hebrew poems celebrating the mutual love of a man and a woman. What is remarkable about these poems is the fact that they focus almost exclusively on the couple's physical delight in each other. Not surprisingly, the very physicality of this book has worried many a biblical scholar in the past and it was common practice to look at it mainly or even solely as an image of God's love for his people Israel and, by implication, for the Church. However, the most recent edition of the Jerusalem Bible treats it first and foremost as a description of human love, as willed and inspired by God.[11]

The Song of Songs does not tell a complete story, rather it shows the feelings, thoughts and actions that happen or are imagined and desired between a man and a woman who are in love and who long to become spouses. The language and imagery belong to a pastoral culture of the fifth or fourth century BC, but the sentiments they express are of all ages and all cultures.[12]

Equal Desire

On re-reading the Song for this book I was struck by how 'modern' it is in its description of the two lovers' equal longing for each other. The woman (the *Beloved*) longs for the man (the *Lover*) just as much as he longs for her. In fact the book opens with the words of the *Beloved*,

> *Let him kiss me with the kisses of his mouth,*
> *for your love-making is sweeter than wine;*
> *delicate is the fragrance of your perfume,*
> *your name is an oil poured out,*
> *and that is why girls love you.* [13]

She goes on to say,

> *I hear my love.*
> *See how he comes*
> *leaping on the mountains,*
> *bounding over the hills.*
> *my love is like a gazelle,*
> *like a young stag.* [14]

He in his turn looks longingly at her,

> *How beautiful you are, my beloved,...*
> *Your eyes are doves, behind your veil ...*
>
> *Your two breasts are like two fawns,*
> *twins of a gazelle,*
> *that feed among the lilies.* [15]

The *Lover* has spoken in language that shows his longing to *touch* her, the *Beloved* longs for him to come to her and *taste* her,

> *Awake, north wind ...*
> *breathe over my garden ...*
> *Let my love come into his garden*
> *let him taste its most exquisite fruits.* [16]

And he says,

> *I come into my garden ...*
> *my promised bride ...*
> *I eat my honey and my honeycomb,*
> *I drink my wine and my milk.*[17]

This is language of the senses, used to express their faithful love for each other.

Although there is no 'story' as such, there is a growing intimacy between the lovers, as we move through the five poems of the Song,

> *How beautiful are your feet in their sandals,*
> *O prince's daughter!*
> *The curve of your thighs is like the curve of a necklace,*
> *work of a master hand.*[18]

This is almost a prayer of thanksgiving, as the 'master hand', of course, is God's.

The girl responds,

> *My love is fresh and ruddy ...*
> *His hands are golden, rounded ...*
> *His belly a block of ivory*
> *covered with sapphires.*[19]

Consummation

The Song of Songs is a collection of poems, some of which are fragments. Many are therefore open to more than one interpretation, but I like to think of the setting for the Epilogue as the time after the consummation of the marriage:

> *Who is this coming from the desert*
> *Leaning on her lover? ...*
> *Set me like a seal on your heart,*
> *Like a seal on your arm.*
> *For love is strong as Death,*

> *Passion as relentless as Sheol. [the Underworld]*
> *The flash of it is a flash of fire,*
> *A flame of Yahweh himself.*[20]

The bride and groom have sought the loneliness of the desert, but they are not entirely alone. Yahweh, God, is with them, and their love is like 'a flame of Yahweh himself'. Indeed, it is Yahweh who has given them the flame which unites them. It is not surprising that extracts from the Song were frequently sung at Jewish marriage feasts.[21]

The Body as the Bearer of Spiritual Intimacy

The Song of Songs concentrates on the physical longing and expression of love, but it is a love which is both spirit and flesh. It is a love which knows how to wait and how to cope in times of trial.

The *Lover* says,

> *I charge you,*
> *daughters of Jerusalem ...*
> *do not rouse, do not wake my beloved*
> *before she pleases.*[22]

The *Beloved* goes looking for the *Lover*, but

> *The watchmen met me ...*
> *They beat me, they wounded me,*
> *they took my cloak away from me ...*[23]

She has risked all by going out alone to search for her lover, and, according to the Jerusalem Bible, the watchmen mistake her for a prostitute. I think there is a deeper meaning to this passage, though: In a society where respectable women, on the whole, did not go out alone, the watchmen see only her outward actions, but not the love that informs them. They are intruders in a world that belongs only to the *Lover* and the *Beloved*. The deeper and the more profound the expression of love, the greater solitude do the lovers need. Only they can enter the Holy of Holies.

The Holy of Holies

A couple making love enter the sanctuary, the 'Holy of Holies' of their marriage both in terms of their shared actions and the room where those actions take place. I remember a lady showing me round her new house, going through all the rooms and then hesitating slightly, before opening the last door, 'This is our bedroom', she said, a little shyly. I could see what was in her mind. 'This is our very private place, our sanctuary, and yet – it is also just a bedroom, so why not show her!'

It is what takes place in the room where we make love that makes it 'holy' and since the bedroom is where a couple usually make love, it becomes special and 'holy' to them. In a very real sense it belongs to them only, it is their secret place.

Self Revelation and Intimacy

I like the philosopher Dietriech von Hildebrand's description of sex as 'the secret of the individual'.[24] Revealing the secret of myself to another person – in full awareness of what I am doing – means that I give myself to that person. I can give no more to anyone. It is the fullness of intimacy.

In the contemporary novel *The Loop*, quoted earlier, Helen enters into a relationship with a much younger man, Luke, after Joel has left her. After she and Luke have begun to live together, Helen reflects on the nature of intimacy, which she feels she is now experiencing for the first time.

To be living with him in that tiny place, which was their world and no one else's, seemed the most natural thing imaginable . . . only now did she realise that there had never been real intimacy [with Joel] of the kind that she shared with Luke. With Joel, she had become watchful of herself, careful at all times to be the kind of woman she thought he wanted and would want to keep.

It seemed to her now that true intimacy was only possible when two people were simply themselves, not constantly monitoring

... for the first time in her life [she felt] completely unjudged.[25]

The book does not try to play down the uncertainty of the future facing the two lovers. Nevertheless, this moving description of their 'togetherness' is true to the very nature of intimacy and therefore also reflects something of the truth about the act of love in marriage.

Trust

The intimacy of an act of love worthy of the name implies great trust, because the man and the woman put off all adornments and defences to give themselves to each other in total nakedness. It is as if they say, 'This is who I am, I give myself to you and I accept your gift to me.'

Looking at the quotations in this and the previous chapter, I have come to realise that they describe the gift of self mainly from the woman's point of view. I suspect that, until recently at least, the gift has been seen very much as the woman's gift to the man, and even the gift of the woman to the man ('Who giveth this woman to be married ...?'[26]).

However, the equal longing of bride and groom in the Song of Songs should not be forgotten. The gift is mutual, so that the man, too, gives himself, though it may not always appear so, even to him.[27] The nakedness, and hence the exposure, associated with the act of love implies great vulnerability. In their mutual self-revelation the man and the woman both become vulnerable, but in different ways.

A woman's vulnerability is more immediately obvious than that of a man. She is, on the whole, physically weaker than the man and, because of her child-bearing role, is especially vulnerable. Her physical make-up and all that it entails makes her gift of self a particular act of trust, which calls on all that is best in a man.[28]

On the other hand, the man, too, becomes vulnerable in the act of love, because he lays aside his strength and becomes open to hurt and rejection. There is therefore a sense in which he becomes even more vulnerable than the woman, because he is normally the one who protects her. A man who gives himself in this way shows great trust and longs for the full acceptance of his gift.

The act of love calls for a very special kind of trust, the trust that only a woman can show to a man and a man to a woman. In circumstances other than those of total trust an act of sex can be a deadly act. That is why Helen felt hurt to the point of suicide, when Joel left her, because he had *known* her, in the full biblical sense of the word, and had rejected her.[29]

Adam *Knew* Eve

Pope John Paul attributed the use of the word *know* for *making love* ('Adam *knew* Eve his wife'[30]) in the original Hebrew of the Old Testament to the limited vocabulary of that language.

On the other hand, as he explained, through this limitation, the Hebrew comes to reveal a profound truth about the meaning of the act of love, because becoming one flesh can indeed be described, and also experienced, as *knowledge*. In the mutual gift of their bodies a man and a woman come to know each other not only as man and woman but as this particular man and woman, uniquely. After many years of marriage a wife might say to her husband, lovingly, 'How well you know me!'

Being Real

Truly knowing someone means being real with that person. I see and love them as they really are and try to show myself to them as I really am. Our relationship can therefore be taken out into the real world without crumbling.

There comes a point in the story of Helen and Luke, when Helen tells him that, as a child, she liked to hide so much that her parents eventually sent her to a psychiatrist, who concluded that she had a problem with reality. Luke realises that she has told him this story, because she wants to tell him that they, too, have a problem with reality.

Luke disagrees, but when he suggests that she should stay with him when he goes to university – she could finish her thesis at the same time! – all Helen says is, 'Oh, Luke . . . I don't know'. They then turn to a different 'language':

> He lowered his head and kissed her and she reached for him and pulled him gently down beside her and he felt their mouths and limbs stir with that mutual, miraculous hunger.
> It was their way now, he realised, his as much as hers. To answer with their bodies those questions too brutal for their heads.[31]

The relationship between Helen and Luke is touching, but also sad, because the expression they give to their love, the complete gift of their bodies, does not correspond to a complete gift of their lives to each other, so that their gift is only a fragment of the whole. The question of their long-term future is still unresolved and remains so at the end of the book.

'I Will'

Opening my 'Holy of Holies' to someone demands a realistic image both of myself and of the person I am thus trusting, and therefore of any future we might have together. It implies an open-ended and unqualified commitment, 'till death us do part'.

The whole of the life of the spouses is underpinned by the consent of the marriage vows, 'will you take this man, will you take this woman . . .'[32] The 'I will' of the marriage vows informs all of married life, even, and perhaps especially, at times when feeling appears absent. It is at such times that a couple recognise that love is indeed 'strong as death' and 'a flame of Yahweh himself'.[33]

As the couple mature, the feelings, which seemed to overwhelm them at the beginning of their marriage, become transparent, enabling husband and wife to see each other with greater clarity. Their lovemaking then becomes a meeting at the very core of their two selves and, for a believer, the realisation grows that God is not only present, but rejoicing in their act of love.

Opening out to Others

When making love, a couple enter into their 'Holy of Holies' and no one else can be present, except God (and perhaps a sleeping baby!). But that does not mean that the couple enter into a kind of 'egoism for two'. What is done in private bears fruit in public, in the couple's relationships with other people, in hospitality and, above all, in children.

Making love can be compared to private prayer: I need the time alone with God, but what has happened in that secret place bears fruit when I go out to meet other people. I will love others better because of what I have learnt while we were alone together. The 'worship' of the body of my beloved also bears fruit. It becomes a union of love, which opens out to others.

Summary

This chapter considers the meaning of the act of love as a physical expression of the spiritual union between husband and wife. It shows that, for men and women, the sexual act is not solely a means of continuing the species, but also, and perhaps principally, a bearer of spiritual intimacy. The act of love is the 'Holy of Holies' of marriage, the unreserved gift of self.

Further Reading

John Paul II, *The Theology of the Body: Human Love in the Divine Plan*, Pauline Books and Media, Boston, 1997. See especially pp. 25-90.

Benedict XVI, *Deus Caritas Est* (God Is Love), Pope Benedict's First Encyclical Letter, Catholic Truth Society, London 2006.

See especially § 6, which contains a succinct commentary on the nature of love in the light of the Song of Songs.

Notes

1 John Paul II, *The Theology of the Body*, p. 81.
2 *The New Jerusalem Bible*, note to Hebrews, 9:2b.
3 Jack Dominian has analysed this concept in much of his work, for instance in *Marriage, Faith and Love*, Collins, Fount Paperbacks, 1981 (*passim*).
4 Nicholas Evans, *The Loop*, Bantam Press, London 1998, p. 68.
5 Adrienne von Speyr, 'Mary in the Church', in *Communio* 20, Summer 1993, pp. 451–6, p. 456. Reprinted by *Communio* (with permission) from *Handmaid of the Lord* tr. E. A. Nelson, San Francisco, Ignatius Press, 1985, pp. 149–55.
6 *The Marriage Service and Nuptial Rite*, p. 5.
7 Elizabeth Jane Howard, *Casting Off*, Pan Books, London 1996 (First published by Macmillan 1995), p. 579.
8 Man kann nicht auf Probe leben, nicht auf Probe lieben, nicht auf Probe sterben.
9 *Catechism of the Catholic Church*, § 2391.
10 See chapter two.
11 *The New Jerusalem Bible*, p. 1028.
12 Ibid., p. 1029.
13 Sg 1:1–3.
14 Sg 2:8.
15 Sg 4:1, 5.
16 Sg 4:16.
17 Sg 5:1.
18 Sg 7:2.
19 Sg 5:10, 14.
20 Sg 8:5, 6.
21 *The New Jerusalem Bible*, p. 1029.
22 Sg 3:5.
23 Sg 5:7.
24 Dietrich von Hildebrand, *In Defence of Purity, An Analysis of the Catholic Ideals of Purity and Virginity*, Sheed and Ward, London 1931, p. 14.
25 Nicholas Evans, *The Loop*, p. 349.
26 Anglican marriage rite, *The Book of Common Prayer*, Cambridge, Cambridge University Press and London, Society for Promoting Christian Knowledge, p. 303 (no date).

27 Pope John Paul II reflects in depth on the meaning of the mutual gift of woman to man and man to woman in relation to Gn 2:23-25. God gave the woman to the man, but also the man to the woman, so that 'He is received as a gift by the woman, in the revelation of . . . the essence of his masculinity, together with the whole truth of his body and sex.' *The Theology of the Body*, p. 72.

28 See chapter two.

29 I am indebted to Mrs Jane Powell for a helpful discussion on this section.

30 Gn 4:1 as quoted by John Paul II in *The Theology of the Body*, p. 78, my italics. I have assumed that the translation is the Pope's own.

31 Nicholas Evans, *The Loop*, pp. 369-70.

32 *The Complete Rite of Marriage*, Catholic Truth Society, p. 34.

33 Sg 8:6.

Chapter Seven

The Gift Bears Fruit

God blessed them, saying to them, 'Be fruitful, multiply, fill the earth and subdue it.'

Genesis 1:28

I did the planting, Apollos did the watering, but God gave growth.

1 Corinthians 3:6

Some friends of mine once told me, 'When we were first married, we had to learn to be with other people'.[1] Their remark struck me very much at the time and has stayed with me over the years. The gift of self, when expressed in its fullest sense as the act of love, obviously requires privacy.[2] Yet it is from this very private and exclusive act that the most important fruit of the marriage springs, as the conception of a child normally takes place within the act of love.

The Gift and its Fruit

The Catechism of the Catholic Church describes marriage as being 'by its nature ordered toward the good of the spouses and the procreation and education of offspring'. It goes on to say that the marriage of a couple who cannot have children can 'radiate a fruitfulness of charity, of hospitality and of sacrifice'.[3] However, this kind of fruitfulness applies to every married couple, whether they are able to have children or not and I would therefore like to begin by saying something about this wider fruitfulness.

The Wider Perspective of Fruitfulness

Work

Some couples are called to bear fruit in a joint undertaking or work. The French-Polish couple Pièrre and Marie Curie come to mind as an exceptional example of fruitful joint work (for which they were to win the Nobel Prize). It was their shared passion for physics that brought them together in the first place and this continued throughout their marriage. When their first daughter was born and Marie Curie published her first independent research in the same year, it was as if one kind of fruitfulness blended in with the other.[4]

Closer to our own times, I have friends whose work within the same subject has been an integral part of their marriage. One of my abiding images of married life is of that couple sitting either side of the fire, both companionably busy with the article they were currently writing. In more recent years the writing pad was exchanged for a laptop, but always there were the glances across the fireplace to see how the other was getting on.

In another setting, a nice couple has just rescued the ailing do-it-yourself shop in our village. She has injected new life into the shop, while he works as a highly reliable builder, conveniently available in the shop from time to time.

In the Service of Others

Some couples find themselves called to bear fruit in 'outreach' to other people. I know of one such couple, both working for an evangelical church, with the wife in particular caring for poor and homeless people. She has written movingly about her gradual involvement in this commitment, which she had to learn to balance against the demands of marriage and family life. The couple's joint availability to the poor is surely an important fruit of their marriage, alongside the children whose care now has to take precedence over, but not exclude, that work.[5]

Hospitality

The American author and Adult R. E. adviser Dolores Leckey
has described a family home, as if seen 'through the
doorway':

> A doorway is a symbol of hospitality. People enter into the inti-
> macy of our homes. It is there that we receive others . . .
>   The experience of God in families happens in the comings
> and goings through our doorways . . . Children are blessed and
> go to school, husbands and wives go to their jobs, and all return
> at the end of the day to seek each other's face. Friends come
> for dinner; sick neighbours are visited. We go to church.[6]

By creating a welcoming home, we receive each other in ever
new ways. We receive God's gifts of children, of friends and
of new forms of service. All this implies openness to what
God will give and an acceptance that we receive all our fruitfulness at his hand.

The Child as Gift

There is a tendency now to think that a couple have the 'right'
to a 'child-free' period at the beginning of a marriage, just as
there is an increasing tendency to assume that a couple have a
'right' to a child, once they want one. As I am writing, the
papers are full of articles about women who find it difficult to
fit children and careers together.[7] It is taken for granted that
the decision when and whether to have children depends solely
on the prospective parents.

   Those who make such assumptions forget that a child is not,
in the final analysis, the property of the couple, but the gift of
God. This point was made, quite unintentionally I am sure, by
a South American woman being interviewed about her life.
When asked about a particular period, she said, 'Then it was
as if God would not give us any more children'. That was
clearly how she thought of having children, as a gift from
God.

   There are many accounts in the Bible, both of very fertile

women, and of women (couples) longing desperately for a child, but, for a long time at least, not being given one. Two stories are particularly poignant, because they involve the birth of a highly significant child to women who were past the age of child-bearing. God had promised Abraham, the 'father' of the Israelite people, that his offspring would be as numerous as the stars in the sky, but Sarah, Abraham's wife, was no longer of child-bearing age, and they had no children. It was not until it was no longer humanly possible for them to have children that Sarah bore a son, Isaac.[8] Something similar happened in the case of the parents of John the Baptist. His mother too, was past child-bearing, when she became pregnant and gave birth to the last and greatest of all the prophets.[9]

These 'impossible' births do not do away with the normal order of conception and childbirth, but they tell us as forcefully as possible, that children are a gift, not a right.[10] We can choose to cooperate with God's creative act, or not, but we cannot ourselves create a child.

How Many Children?

Church Teaching

Although the much-quoted documents *Gaudium et* Spes (1965)[11] and *Humanae Vitae* (1968)[12] speak of the need to limit family size, they still emphasise the virtues of having a large family. Thus *Humanae Vitae* speaks with particular approval of those who make

> the deliberate and generous decision to raise a numerous family,

though it makes it clear that it is aware of the difficulties in doing so.[13]

Pope John Paul's *Familaris Consortio* (1981)[14] does not explicitly single out a large family for praise. However, in his reflections on the Theology of the Body in 1984, the Pope quotes the above passage from *Humanae Vitae* as normative.[15] In fairness it has to be said that both *Gaudium et Spes* and

Humanae Vitae speak of 'responsible parenthood' as applying not only to those who decide to aim for a large family, but also for those who, with due consideration of all relevant factors, aim at a smaller family.[16]

It is significant that the *Catechism of the Catholic Church*, published in 1994, tones down the praise of a large family somewhat. It merely says that 'Sacred Scripture and the Church's traditional practice see in *large families* a sign of God's blessing and the parents' generosity.'[17] However, in their recent document *Cherishing Life* (2004) the Catholic Bishops of England and Wales do not mention a specific family size as ideal, but rather stress the importance of parents caring for their children and educating them in 'what is most worthwhile and valuable in life'.[18] Thus the emphasis is on the quality of family life, rather than the large families of earlier times and different forms of society.

It seems to me that the deciding factor for any couple about the intended size of their family must be love: Their love and care for each other, their love for any children they already have and, not to be forgotten, for the world into which new children will be born. All of these considerations can act as pointers to God's will for this particular couple.

The Gift of Self and Family Planning

In our times, with our greater understanding of human fertility, every couple face decisions about family planning, which entail specific actions either to avoid or to seek conception. Most people today take it for granted that such decisions rest with the couple alone, so that the Church's teaching about openness to new life and its rejection of contraception is one of the most hotly debated issues both inside and outside the Catholic Church.

Avoiding Conception

I remember vividly the moment when the encyclical *Humanae Vitae*, which clarified church teaching on the moral status of contraceptives, was made public in the summer of 1968. I was taking part in a Catholic residential course in the countryside near Copenhagen and the Danish equivalent of the BBC immediately descended, wanting to interview a doctor participant who had been much involved in the public debate on the subject. I can still see him walking across the grass towards the waiting journalists, very slowly, and I remember thinking, 'He is giving himself time to pray.'

The expectation, among Catholics too, had been that the document would find at least the pill morally acceptable. The doctor was one of the few people who had spoken up for the teaching expressed in the encyclical and who did so again on the broadcast. Later on, at a hastily convened meeting of the course participants, he spoke in favour of the Church's teaching once more, but again, the majority was up in arms at what was seen as a prohibition too far.

When I returned to my job in Britain later that year, I found that the response of British Catholics had been very similar. The reaction of the author and broadcaster Libby Purves, who distanced herself from the Church largely because of this issue, was typical of many. In her autobiography she said that it was one thing for the Church to ask people to wait till they were married before having intercourse, quite another to ask them to do even more waiting after they were married – unless they wanted ten children![19]

My own reaction, and this was shortly to become an issue for me too, as I married in 1970, was one of overall agreement with the principles of *Humanae Vitae*, but with a sense of unease, because it seemed to me that it could have spoken more convincingly, though it may have said all that was possible at the time.

The encyclical describes married love beautifully:

> *Total* that is to say, it is a very special form of personal friendship in which husband and wife generously share everything.[20]

It also states that every act of intercourse must be open to new life, since depriving it of its (potential) fertility would

... contradict the nature of both man and of woman and of their most intimate relationship.[21]

When discussing this passage with others, I have often come across comments to the effect that it is nonsense to speak of always being open to new life, since new life is only possible when a woman is fertile, and even women of child-bearing age have infertile as well as fertile phases in their monthly cycles. Obviously, a woman can only conceive when she is fertile. I therefore think the passage needs 'unpacking' to the effect that 'intercourse must be open to new life, *when such life is possible*'. It does not make sense to speak of being open to new life, when, by ordinary human reckoning, conception is impossible, because the wife, or the husband, is infertile. But nor does it make sense to speak as if we know or can do everything. The encyclical is asking couples to plan responsibly, but, having planned, to leave the outcome in God's hands.

Giving All that I Owe You

The act of love expresses the total gift of self of husband and wife. It must therefore be given and accepted without reserve: 'This is me as I am at this moment, this is you as you are at this moment.' Contraceptives shut out part of that gift, because, in different ways, they all tamper with the truth about the gift. This can be seen most clearly with the various 'barrier' methods, which are just that, 'barriers', often introduced at the very moment of gift. The pill is less obtrusively interfering, but it still means that the woman gives herself, not as she is, but in an artificially induced infertile state.

I was interested to find that, once I was married, the thought of using any kind of 'barrier' seemed totally unacceptable, not just in theory, but through my experience of what it meant to make love. When I was, briefly, prescribed the pill for non-contraceptive reasons, I also came to realise that I did not like making use of its contraceptive side effect, because it felt as if an alien element had been introduced into my relationship with my husband.

Thus far I was in agreement with *Humanae Vitae*, but in the English translations of the Latin original that I have seen, the encyclical goes on to say that contraceptive intercourse is 'intrinsically wrong' or 'intrinsically dishonest' – depending on which translation is used.[22] These are harsh words, since, surely, couples using contraceptives do not mean to be 'wrong' and certainly not 'dishonest'. It therefore seemed worth consulting the Latin of the original, which has *intrinsece inhonestum*.[23]

With the help of a Latinist theologian, I discovered that, though *intrinsece* means approximately the same as the English 'intrinsically', *inhonestum* does not, as the English speaker might think, mean *dishonest*, but rather 'lacking in or failing to give due honour'. 'Dishonest' is therefore a misleading translation, whereas 'wrong', though better, fails to capture the full meaning of *inhonestum*. In marriage, husband and wife *honour* each other with their bodies, as the Anglican rite of marriage beautifully puts it. A couple who have contraceptive intercourse do not give themselves in a way that honours the other person fully. What is more, a gift of 'less than all' between husband and wife is in itself 'failing in due honour', regardless of how the couple think or feel about it, just as inhaling asbestos dust is damaging to health, whether I know about it or not. The encyclical, therefore, expresses a truth about the nature of the act of love which is offered to everyone not just to Catholics.[24]

None of this was clear to me on my first reading of the document all those years ago, but, as already mentioned, my own experience of married life has confirmed the essential teaching of *Humanae Vitae* and has been further affirmed by later documents on the subject.

The Theology of the Body

The understanding of the meaning of the gift of self, which I have gradually gained in the course of married life, has been underpinned in recent years by the Theology of the Body taught, above all, by Pope John Paul II.[25] This teaching with its emphasis on the total gift in truth rather than 'the two purposes of the marriage act', has, so to speak, put flesh on the teaching of *Humanae Vitae*.[26] When husband and wife enter the holy place of their lovemaking, they can only do so in a way that is worthy of the other person (and of God), if they give themselves in complete truth.

Part of this truth is that the female cycle has both fertile and infertile phases. I see this naturally occurring pattern as an invitation from the Creator to responsible cooperation with him, both in seeking and in avoiding conception. Living according to this pattern means always giving the gift in truth and for me that is the compelling reason for accepting the teaching of the Church on this matter.

Living the Teaching

Natural Family Planning

Living the teaching of the Church means making use of what is generally known as Natural Family Planning (NFP). As is well known, this method relies on the wife's recording of her body temperature and other physical signs of (in)fertility and the sharing of this information with her husband, so that they can decide when it is right for them to make love.[27] NFP encourages and builds on that good communication between the spouses, which is necessary for every aspect of married life.

There is evidence, particularly in recent years, that some couples who use this method find it both supportive of their marriage and practically reliable, but there are also those who speak of considerable difficulties in living with NFP.[28]

Objections

Objections to NFP centre around two problems: its perceived ineffectiveness and, as we have seen, 'the waiting'. Someone once said to me, 'People who practise NFP turn into parents!' She meant, of course, that they would have unplanned babies, but this need not be so. A recent independent study has shown that NFP, when consistently and correctly used, can be as effective as the pill.[29] I also think that one has to balance the need to make love against the consequences of conceiving a child and different couples will need to make different decisions. A couple with strong motivation and serious reasons for not conceiving are likely to use NFP in a different way to a husband and wife who would not mind having another child.

On the other hand, there is no denying that a certain amount of waiting is necessary for a couple who do not want to conceive. Waiting is something we are not very good at these days, but waiting can mean longing and a great joy in the fulfilment of what we wait for. As one respondent to a questionnaire put it:

> Other methods of family planning take sex for granted. This one makes it very special.[30]

This added appreciation does not mean that the longing and waiting is always easy, or that every couple who try NFP now is satisfied with it (as can be seen, for instance, from the comments at the *Listening 2004* meeting quoted in chapter one and from ongoing correspondence in the *Tablet*[31]), but it does mean that love can grow even, and perhaps especially, when immediate sexual satisfaction is not possible. It is also important to be aware that there are times in every marriage when choosing *not* to make love is the most loving action. I am thinking not only of the times when planning another child would be irresponsible, but also of periods when the husband or wife is ill or exhausted, or simply does not wish to express love in this way. The loving choice not to make love, even when the act of love could be engaged in, can pave the way for showing love when the act may no longer be possible and I will return to this in chapter thirteen.

Truth as the Last Word

Much of the debate about NFP has centred on its level of effectiveness compared with the various methods of contraception and on the satisfaction or otherwise of couples using it. It is therefore easy to forget that, fundamentally, the question is not about effectiveness or satisfaction, important though these are, but about truth.

If it is true, now, that we may only engage in the act of love as we are at the time, without contraceptive barriers, then that has always been true. The effectiveness or ineffectiveness of any given method of family planning does not alter that. The difference, in our times, is that we have discovered more of the truth about our bodies, so that we can use this knowledge to help regulate the conception of children. Our deepening understanding of the human body can be compared to the development of the Church's teaching through the ages that we looked at in chapter four. As with doctrine, the whole picture has always been there, but a more penetrating light is now shining on it.

When the Spouses do not Agree

When one spouse wishes to practise family planning according to the teaching of the Church and the other does not, a particularly difficult situation arises. In 1997 the Pontifical Council for the Family published a document on this question, mainly aimed at confessors but also for married couples.

The document includes some guidelines for couples, addressed particularly to the marriage partner who wishes to follow the teaching of the Church, but, through him or her, also to the other partner. It states that cooperation in contraceptive practice in such a case 'can be licit (permissible) when the three following conditions are jointly met':

1. when the action of the cooperating spouse is not already illicit in itself;
2. when proportionally grave reasons exist for cooperating in the sin of the other spouse;
3. when one is seeking to help the other spouse to desist from such conduct (patiently, with prayer, charity and dialogue; although not necessarily in that moment, nor on every single occasion).[32]

In other words, the 'cooperating spouse' is asked to do what is humanly possible to comply with the teaching of the Church, while preserving the unity of the marriage.

Doing something that is 'illicit in itself' would be, for instance, for a husband or wife to use contraceptives at the request of the other spouse. There is a difference between making love to a marriage partner who uses a contraceptive, because he or she does not agree with or understand the teaching of the Church, and doing so oneself.

It is interesting that the same document exhorts a priest hearing confession

> To avoid demonstrating a lack of trust either in the grace of God or in the dispositions of the penitent, by exacting humanly impossible absolute guarantees of irreproachable future conduct.[33]

The last passage refers to a man or woman confessing contraceptive practice rather than cooperating in it, but it is another instance of the fundamental attitude of patience, love and trust (surely greatly developed in recent times) which the Church encourages both clergy and married couples to have with regard to these sensitive issues.

Hard Cases

There are many kinds of 'hard cases', but I would like to mention just a few that seem particularly hard.

1. Breakdown in Communication

The practice of NFP relies on good communication and understanding between husband and wife, but there are cases where this has never existed or has broken down. A friend of mine drew my attention to the most extreme case of such breakdown. 'What if the husband forces himself on the wife,' she said, 'so that she has child after child until her health breaks down and she can care neither for the children nor herself?' 'In such a case,' I said (and she had apparently known several), 'I think we are talking about protection against the effects of rape and I do not think it would be wrong for her to use some form of contraception.' One must add that, in this sad situation, the survival of the marriage itself is clearly in question.

2. Risk to Marriage Partner or Child

The most commonly quoted situations, where every reasonable action must be taken to avoid conception, are those in which the wife's health (or life) would be at risk from another pregnancy, or where there is a serious inherited disease in the family. These cases are more difficult than those of 'ordinary' families, because the consequences of family planning 'failure' are much more serious. However, the choice between contraception and 'gift in truth' is the same and couples in this situation need the very best medical and ethical advice and information, in order to make the decisions that are right for them.

It is not possible to discuss 'hard cases' without mentioning HIV and AIDS, although the problems of living with these conditions go beyond the scope of this book. I therefore only want to comment on the case of a married couple, one of whom is HIV positive or has AIDS. In this situation there is the problem not only of infecting any children of the marriage, but also of passing on a life-threatening disease to the other spouse. It is therefore not a case of restricting intercourse to those times when conception is impossible, but of the act of intercourse itself being a likely cause of the transmission of a life-threatening infection. The use of a condom to protect from infection in this situation is therefore advocated by many, though to date the Church has argued against this, because of the contraceptive properties of the condom. In a recent document the Bishops of England and Wales, taking into account both practical and theological considerations, said that,

> the only assured way to prevent passing on [HIV/AIDS] is to express love in ways other than through sexual intercourse.[34]

It is significant that this passage comes form a section entitled 'Not doing harm', which speaks of 'not carelessly inflicting harm on others'.[35] It is well known that condoms are not fail proof, so that there are good practical reasons for not risking the consequences of such failure. However, there are also theological reasons for not exposing another person, let alone your spouse, to the risk of death. In its interpretation of the Fifth Commandment, 'You shall not kill', the *Catechism* states,

> Life and physical health are precious gifts entrusted to us by God. We must take reasonable care of them, taking into account the needs of others and the common good.[36]

Taking care of life and health means not only our own health, but that of others. This obligation, in my view, is the central theological reasons why a husband and wife, one of whom is infected with HIV/AIDS, are called 'to express love in ways other than through sexual intercourse'.

3. Mental Illness

The use of the pill to treat organic disease is considered acceptable by the Church since, in this case, it is not prescribed for contraceptive reasons.[37] However, if a woman suffers from serious mental illness and cannot, for the moment, 'manage' NFP, could a contraceptive not be used to help reduce anxiety, thus providing her and her husband with a 'safe' space in which to make love? I do not think such a decision would show lack of trust in God, but rather a realisation that there is a limit to how many problems a couple can deal with at any one time.

When Conception Is Impossible

Most couples want the gift of self to bear fruit in a child and for most a child or children do come along at some point. On the other hand, there are couples who remain childless, no matter how hard they 'try for a baby'. That does not mean that their mutual gift does not bear fruit, because, as we have seen, there are many other ways in which a couple can be fruitful, in charitable work, for instance, or in joint research, or large-scale hospitality.

The right (or otherwise) of couples to exclude the possibility of conception from intercourse has been debated over many years, but it is only comparatively recently that their right to conceive a child outside the act of love has come into focus. The new techniques of fertilising an egg outside the womb have made it possible for couples to have children they could not otherwise have had. However, as we have seen in chapter three, this procedure, which can look so inviting, fragments not only the act of love, but also in some cases, as for instance with donor egg or sperm, the link between child and parents. The child was much wanted, but did that give the parents the right to try to conceive by *any* means?

Sometimes a couple turn to adoption in order to have a family. Why is adoption not a fragmentation of the act of love? After all, the adopted child is not genetically that of the adoptive parents. I think there is a difference between adoption and the various forms of assisted conception, because the mutual gift of the parents is not interfered with. In such a case the love of husband and wife bears fruit in their wish to provide a home for a child, whose own parents were unable to care for it and their love reaches out to and includes the adopted child. Something similar can happen when one or both spouses already have children before the marriage. In this situation the couple can welcome the children with a special kind of hospitality, which includes them in the life of the new family.

Contrasting Couples

There are as many different ways of living a marriage as there are couples. A friend of mine once said that there is a sliding scale, with 'strong emphasis on mutual gift' at one end and 'strong emphasis on children' at the other.[38] Both 'gift' and 'openness to children' need to be present in a marriage, but not always in the same proportion and the emphasis can shift from one phase of the same marriage to another.

I have known two couples who, for me, represent the opposite ends of the scale. One of these had ten children, all lovingly brought up in a chaotic house, which was forever having bits added on to it. The parents always had time for their children, for serious discussion and for prayer, but keeping the house tidy was not a priority and that was how they coped. Living in a household of this kind would have driven some people to insanity, but I think it worked for this couple, who had made a conscious choice to have a large family and to live the way they did.

The other couple, both teachers, were unable to have children and were not physically and psychologically strong, but their happy marriage bore fruit through their teaching and in out-of-school activities with the children they taught. Most marriages are somewhere between these two extremes and no two are alike.

In a discussion of the difficulties and pitfalls of clerical marriage, the former Anglican Bishop of Liverpool, David Sheppard, threw interesting light on the balancing act of married life,

> I am convinced that married partnerships cannot thrive without making prime time for each other and not just the fag end of the day or the week.[39]

I think his words can be applied to all married couples, both wives and husbands. There are choices to be made about work and family time, but also about family and 'couple time'. In this connection it becomes clear that the double purpose of the act of love, that of uniting the couple and of bearing fruit, applies to the whole of the marriage union. There has to be time for the children and other 'fruit' of the marriage, but also for that private communion between husband and wife, in which the creativeness of the marriage is rooted.

A Final Word: Taking or Receiving

Producing fruit, of whatever kind, involves waiting and waiting always has an element both of uncertainty and of openness. Believers wait for what God will give and there is the unexpected child as well as the unexpected lack of a child.

In the wider perspective of fruitfulness there is also the unexpected invitation to bear witness to a particular kind of family life. When my husband and I saw the film about Ghandi, we were much struck by the action of his parents (well-to-do 'Anglicised' Indians), who decided at a certain

point in the Indian fight for independence that they must start
wearing Indian clothes all the time. So they burnt their Savile
Row suits and began to 'wear' their Indian identity. I wonder
if this was what later enabled Ghandi to adopt the way of life,
and dress, of the poorest of the poor? If Ghandi's courage was
the fruit of his parents' sacrifice, then surely that courage was
also a fruit of their marriage.

God gives, we receive. At times that means accepting a
hard or difficult fruit of the gift of self. Such a fruit is a
reminder that a willingness to suffer (often forgotten) is also
part of the mutual gift of self and, in some way, always the
condition for the bearing of fruit.

Summary

The gift of self in marriage is always fruitful. The child is the
supreme but not the only fruit of married love. This chapter
shows that the call to fruitfulness is a call to trusting and
responsible cooperation with the will of God and that every
couple is called in a unique way. The chapter discusses
general objections to Natural Family Planning as well as
'difficult cases' and the problems of those who cannot
conceive. It explains that the teaching of the Church on
responsible parenthood is rooted in the meaning of the gift of
self as a total and unreserved gift.

Further Reading

Humanae Vitae, On Human Life, Encyclical Letter of Pope
Paul VI, Catholic Truth Society, London 1968.

Donum Vitae, Instruction on Respect for Human Life in its
Origin and on the Dignity of Procreation, Congregation for
the Doctrine of the Faith, Catholic Truth Society, London
1987.
Contains official Church teaching on biomedical research. See
especially Part II, 'Interventions upon Human Procreation'.

John Paul II, *Evangelium Vitae*, Encyclical Letter on the Value and Inviolability of Human Life, Catholic Truth Society, London 1995.
See especially §§ 42–3 entitled 'Be fruitful, multiply, fill the earth and subdue it' (Gn 1:28).

Why Humanae Vitae Was Right: A Reader, (ed.) Janet E. Smith, Ignatius Press, San Francisco 1993.
Contains a particularly helpful article on 'The Moral Use of Natural Family Planning' by Janet E. Smith (who teaches philosophy at the University of Dallas), and also an annotated list of translations of *Humanae Vitae* and a new translation of this document by Janet E. Smith (p. 533).

Robert Blair Kaiser, *The Encyclical That Never Was: The Story of the Pontifical Commission on Population, Family and Birth, 1964–1966*. Sheed & Ward, London 1985, 1987.
Describes the origin and history of the Commission which reported to Pope Paul VI on birth control issues. Contains the 'Majority Report', which advised the Pope to change the Church's teaching on contraception. Argues for a change in church teaching on contraception.

Kimberly Hahn, *Life-Giving Love*, Charis Books 2002, ISBN 0813209412.
The author, who is a married woman and mother, writes in support of the teaching of *Humanae Vitae* and explains the meanng of NFP in the context of married life.

Notes

1 Anita Dowsing, *A Marriage in Our Time*, Sheed and Ward, London 2000, p. 99.
2 I am grateful to Rev. Tony Ranzetta for pointing out that such privacy is not always available in overcrowded households, for instance if sharing a house with the in-laws, or in some Third World countries, where the couple may not have a room of its own.
3 *The Catechism of the Catholic Church*, §§ 1601, 1654.
4 Eve Curie, *Madame Curie*, The Biography by her Daughter, (tr.)

Vincent Sheean, first published 1938. Many reprints, Mercury Edition 1962, Heineman, London Melbourne, Toronto, esp. p. 158.

5 Philippa Stroud with Christine Leonard, *God's Heart for the Poor*, Kingsway Publications, Eastbourne 1999, esp. pp. 195–200.

6 Dolores R. Leckey, *The Ordinary Way*, A Family Spirituality, Crossroad, New York 1987, pp. 144–5.

7 See for instance, 'The Cruel choice' in *The Times*, Tuesday April 23 2002.

8 Gn 15:5; 21:1–7.

9 Lk 1:24.

10 *The Catechism of the Catholic Church*, § 2378.

11 'The Church in the Modern World' (*Gaudium et Spes*), in Vatican Council II, The Conciliar and Post Conciliar Documents, (ed.) Austin Flannery OP, Dominican Publications, Dublin, 7th Printing, July 1984.

12 *Of Human Life* (*Humanae Vitae*), Encyclical Letter of His Holiness Pope Paul VI, in John Paul II, *The Theology of the Body*.

13 'Church in the Modern World' para. 50; *Humanae Vitae* (Of Human Life) Appendix, p. 432, §§ 2, 10.

14 *The Christian Family in the Modern World*, Catholic Truth Society, London.

15 John Paul II, *The Theology of the Body*, p. 394. (The reflections were written in 1984, but published with other material on the Theology of the Body in 1994).

16 Ibid., p. 394.

17 *Catechism of the Catholic Church*, § 2373. The emphasis is in the original.

18 The Bishops' Conference of England and Wales, *Cherishing Life*, Catholic Truth Society, London, 2004, §9.

19 Libby Purves, *Holy Smoke*, pp. 133–8.

20 *Humanae Vitae* (Of Human Life) Encyclical Letter of His Holiness Pope Paul VI, in John Paul II, *The Theology of the Body*, Appendix, p. 432, § 9. My emphasis.

21 Ibid., Appendix, p. 432, § 12.

22 Ibid., §14. The translation printed in John Paul II, *The Theology of the Body*, has 'dishonest', whereas the remaining translations I have consulted all have 'wrong'. (These are: The Catholic Truth Society, London 1970; Ignatius Press, San Francisco 1998 and the one in Janet E. Smith (ed. and translator) *in Why*

Humanae Vitae Was Right, A Reader, Ignatius Press, San Francisco 1993 and the English translation on the Vatican website.

23 The Latin version of *Humanae Vitae* is available on the Vatican website: http://www.vatican.va
Go to 'Encyclicals', then 'Humanae Vitae', then choose Latin.

24 I am indebted to Fr Simon Blakesley, MCL, JCL, VJ for drawing my attention to the problems of translating this phrase and to Fr Jerome Bertram, CO, MA, FSA for helping me with the translation and interpretation.

25 John Paul II, *The Theology of the Body*, especially pp. 388 and 396.

26 Ibid., p. 422.

27 Fertility indicators other than body temperature are cervical mucus and other cervical changes. See Hanna Klaus MD 'Action, Effectiveness and Medical Side-Effects of Common Methods of Family Planning', p. 4. Secretariat for Pro-Life Activities, United States conference of Catholic Bishops, 3211 4th Street, NE, Washington, DC 20017–1194 (202)541–3070, November 2002. Available on http://www.usccb.org/prolife /action.htm. See also Dr Elizabeth Clubb and Jane Knight, *Fertility*, A Comprehensive Guide to Natural family Planning, David and Charles, Newton Abbot, Devon, 1992, p. 34ff.

28 The digest of Current Medical Research on the US Catholic Bishops' web site quotes a number of studies on levels of satisfaction with NFP, not all of them from Catholic sources. The levels of satisfaction range from 66% to 97% for men and from 72% to 98% for women. The highest levels of satisfaction came from a World health Organisation study of 1987. http://www.usccb.org/prolife/cmrwinsp02.htm 'NFP and Marital Dynamics', p. 15ff. John Marshall, who was member of the commission which advised Pope Paul VI to change the Church's teaching on contraception, has written an article summarising his experience as a commission member and his objections to teaching of *Humanae Vitae*.: 'My Voyage of Discovery', in *The Tablet* 23 November 2002, pp. 8–9. The author was a medical adviser to the (then) Catholic Marriage Advisory Council and had carried out medical research into NFP.
Referring to a straw poll of *Tablet* readers using NFP, Annabel Miller quotes both satisfied and dissatisfied couples. See 'How Natural Is NFP?' in *The Tablet*, 2 December 2000, pp. 1632–4.

29 University of California, Davis Campus, Health Education Program, 'Contraceptive Options', 2004. http://healthcenter .ucdavis.edu/topics/contraception/efficacy.html According to this study 'perfect' use of the method was 98% safe (about the same as the pill), whereas 'typical' use of NFP was 80% safe. The UK family Planning Association gives the same figure for perfect use of the method (2004). See http://www.thefword .org.uk/reviews/2004/06/taking_charge_of_your_fertility .

30 Annabel Miller, 'How Natural Is NFP?', in *The Tablet*, 2 December 2000, p. 1633.

31 See for instance, P. P. McCarthy's Letter in *The Tablet*, 24 July 2004 and also negative comments in Annabel Miller's article quoted above.

32 '*Vademecum* for Confessors on some Themes of Conjugal Morality', in *Briefing,* vol. 27, issue 3, 20 March 1997, p. 38.

33 Ibid.

34 Catholic Bishops' Conference of England and Wales, *Cherishing Life*, para. 170.

35 Ibid., § 167.

36 *Catechism of the Catholic Church*, § 2288.

37 *On Human Life, 'Humanae Vitae'*, §15.

38 I am indepbted to Professor Margaret Spufford for suggesting this image to me.

39 David Sheppard and Derek Worlock, *Better Together*, Hodder and Stoughton Ltd. 1988, pp. 30-1.

Chapter Eight

Christ's Gift of Self to the Church – and the Gift in Marriage

All deep love seeks union.
Ruth Burrows[1]

This is why a man leaves his father and mother and becomes
attached to his wife, and the two become one flesh.[2] *This mystery*
has great significance, but I am applying it to Christ and the
Church.

Ephesians 5:31-2

Good Friday

The liturgy of the Catholic Church on Good Friday is stark. The congregation gathers in silence in a church stripped of every decoration, facing a bare altar, without candles or flowers. The priests too enter in silence and prostrate themselves before the empty altar. Everyone in the congregation kneels to join in their prostration.

What Christ did for all of us when he died on the Cross is beyond words and the silent prostration seems the only fitting way of showing at least some awareness of his gift. It is also a way of expressing, in a language which echoes that of his gift, our willingness to give ourselves in return, to him and to other people, in response to his unique act of love.

All in the Church share in the events of Christ's life through the liturgy, but married couples live Christ's gift of himself to the Church in a special way, since his love for the Church is likened to that of a bridegroom for his bride.[3]

An 'Ordinary Wedding' and Christ's Gift

There is a link between Christ's gift of himself to the Church at the Last Supper and on Good Friday and what happens in an ordinary human marriage. At the Last Supper Christ 'vows' himself to the Church through the gift of himself under the 'veiled' form of bread and wine. The meal is a celebration of this gift, but, as with an ordinary marriage, the gift is not complete until it has been consummated. Christ's gift was 'consummated' on the Cross, when he gave himself in his human form, 'unveiled', as at the consummation of a marriage.

Christ's last words from the Cross before he died were 'It is fulfilled';[4] his ministry was complete, he had given himself as fully as a bridegroom gives himself to his bride. 'This is my body, it is for you'.[5]

A Double Image

The biblical writers have used the language of married love to speak of God's (Christ's) love for his people and, by implication, for all mankind, both in the Old and the New Testaments. But the image does not begin with these writers. It has its origin in God's will to create men and women in his likeness and to invite them to become one flesh and become fruitful.[6]

When St Paul, quoting Genesis, speaks of the mystery of husband and wife becoming one flesh, he sees in it a prophesy of the marriage of Christ and the Church. The Christ-Church marriage is therefore envisaged from the very beginning. Since men and women, and hence marriage, have been created with the Christ-Church marriage in mind, human marriage is taken into the very heart of Christ's gift to the Church and of God's love for all mankind.

Like all images, that of the Church as the bride of Christ has to be used with care and not be pushed too far. The function of the image is precisely to point to a reality which is beyond words (that is why we use an image!) and to give a 'flavour' of what we cannot convey in any other way.[7]

Clearly the relationship between God and his people is not the same as an ordinary human marriage. For one thing it is not a marriage of equals, but a marriage through which God *bestows* equality on his bride, the Church, if she will but accept his gift. The acceptance of the gift implies a willingness to follow Christ through joy as well as pain, even the pain of 'crucifixion'.

For Better for Worse

The word 'crucifixion' can be understood in other ways than the literal one of being nailed to a cross. It can be used figuratively about being tied to something or someone in a painful way. In spite of this, I was taken aback when, during a discussion about marriage and Christ's gift of self, a priest said to me that, in a sense, the partners are *crucified* to each other. 'What do you mean?' I said, and then he went on to explain and I understood. 'When they marry,' he said, 'a man and woman are bound to each other, come what may. Their vocation to lifelong marriage means a call to accept and transform in love, whatever difficulties come their way, whether of personality, from external trials such as poverty or illness, or the sorrow of a child who seems beyond help. The gift in marriage does not *seek* the Cross, it is fundamentally given in joy, but the way ahead passes through dark places, where pain rather than joy is what is *felt*. It is the acceptance of the other in pain as well as joy that makes for lifelong fidelity and only God can give a couple the strength to do this. For the Christian this means a deliberate turning to the Cross; for all married couples it means persevering, whatever the cost.'

Contemplating Christ on the Cross

Someone once said to me that she could not bear to look at a crucifix, because of the reality of what it depicted. In our times in particular there is a tendency to reject anything that is difficult or painful and it is indeed hard to gaze unflinchingly at the Cross.

The outward reality is that of a man nailed to a piece of rough wood, in full view of every passer-by. The man is naked, like a lover, but without any of the joy and pleasure of the act of love; on the contrary, he is in the most terrible pain, dying the death allotted to common criminals. This is Christ's final, total gift of self. In his nakedness he is without defence against the indifference and rejection of the people (Israel) he had come to save; no loving arms around him, only two faithful followers at the foot of the Cross, Mary, his mother, and John, his disciple, representing the New people of God, the Church.

This is the *kind* of love that married couples are meant to have for each other and which the Song of Songs describes when it shows the woman (*the Beloved*) going out in search of her *Lover*, thereby risking her reputation (she is taken for a 'loose woman') and perhaps even her life ('They beat me . . .')[8]

Christ's gift of self says something fundamental about the commitment in marriage that is often forgotten. It is rooted in the will to give, not in emotions.

An Example

There is no life without a 'cross', nor is there a marriage in which the Cross does not make itself felt, though more poignantly so in some marriages than in others. The Soviet Jews Anatoly and Avital Shcharansky had been married for only a short time, when he was imprisoned in the (then) Soviet Union for campaigning for human rights for his fellow Jews in that country.

Far from giving up on the marriage, he remained faithful in his prison cell and his wife spent the next eleven years fighting for his release, touring the world speaking about their plight and appealing to every official body she could think of. Letters between them were few and far between, yet they never lost hope.

Their fidelity – and faith! the two words are related linguistically) – was rewarded when Anatoly (who later changed his

name to Nathan) was finally released in 1986 and was allowed
to settle with his wife in (modern) Israel. Only then were they
able to begin married life proper, to make a home and have
children. Their love and patience had truly been tested and to
me as a Christian the moving story of their faithful love
speaks not only of Christ's suffering and death, but also of his
Resurrection.

Nor were those years wasted. After his release Anatoly
said,

> Believe me when I say it simply, those long years apart were
> worth living, truly. It was a hard period of life, but also respon-
> sible and . . . impressive for us both.[9]

No marriage thus tested could survive on feeling only (indeed
can any marriage!) but the 'resurrection' element in this
marriage is as important as the 'Cross'. It is a reminder that
suffering does not have the final word, that Christ contem-
plated his final self surrender with joy as well as anguish[10] and
that the joy of the Resurrection was the final word for him, as
it will be for us and I will return to this subject in chapter thirteen.

Marriage: the Eternal Dimension

Every Christian marriage is an image of Christ's faithful love
for the Church, but the comparison between Christian
marriage and the love of Christ for the Church seems easier
to understand in cases where husband and wife have been
married once only. Yet widows and widowers are free to, and
do, remarry. How is it possible to understand such marriages
in the light of the one marriage of Christ to the Church?

It seems to me that each marriage represents a different and
unique way of living Christ's love for the Church. Every
marriage lived in Christ adds to the eternal dimension and the
fullness of the gift of Christ to the Church and of the Church
to Christ. The same person can therefore add to this fullness
through more than one marriage, though that would not be the
call of every widowed person.

Marriage Taken up into the Gift of the Church

For a married couple the gift of their bodies to each other also implies a gift to Christ, to the extent that they want to follow him in their married life. The gift then becomes a 'double gift', a gift to each other in the love of Christ, and a gift to Christ as part of the Church's gift to him.

As members of the Church married couples share in the Church's 'yes' to Christ, which he is waiting for in each one of us, whatever our vocation, and which will be said, in its fullness, at the end of time.[11]

The Eucharist and the Act of Love

Christ's gift of self on the Cross was definitive and unrepeatable, but he continues to give himself under the form of bread and wine, at every celebration of the Mass. In the Eucharist his gift is made available to every member of the Church in every age. But it is not only Christ who gives himself at the Eucharist, every member of the congregation is invited to give themselves to him in return and, through him, to all others.

The Eucharist resembles the act of love in that it is not celebrated once only but is repeated again and again during the life time of the Church to make the Church's gift to Christ ever more profound and ever more perfect. The Eucharist is the 'Holy of Holies' in the Church's life, just as the act of love is the 'Holy of Holies' of a marriage and nourishes and deepens the love of husband and wife.[12]

The time between the death and resurrection of Christ and his Second Coming at the end of time can be described as the time of his 'marriage' with the Church and every member of the Church is called to live this 'marriage' not only in the joy of the Eucharist, but also through accepting the pain of the Cross, whatever form it takes for them.

Living the Cross

Married couples live the 'yes' of their vows every day of their lives, whatever pain and hardship they meet through it. In so doing, they prepare for their final 'yes' to Christ at the time of their deaths, but they also share in the repeated 'yes' of the Church, the Bride of Christ, to her Bridegroom, because, during the time of their marriage, they live a small portion of the 'marriage' of the Church.

This is true even when one 'half' of the couple does not believe, because all who 'sincerely follow all that is right'[13] and accept whatever suffering comes their way are in fact following Christ and will be given strength to persevere, with their spouses, to the end.

Summary

This chapter likens Christ's gift of self on the Cross to the consummation of a marriage. Consummation is the moment of irrevocable gift of self, for Christ on the Cross, for married couples in the act of love. The Cross is a reminder that the physical gift of self in marriage is rooted in the will to give, not in the pleasure and joy that normally accompany the act of love.

Further Reading

The Sunday Missal, Collins Liturgical Publications, August 1975.
Includes the liturgy for Good Friday.

Karl Rahner, *The Eternal Year*, (tr.) John Shea, SS, London, Burns and Oates, 1964.
The chapter on *Advent* (pp. 13–19) provides helpful reading on the relationship between time before and after the birth of Christ and eternity.

J. M. Lustiger, *The Mass*, (tr.) Rebecca Howell Balinski,

Collins, Fount Paperbacks, London 1990.
Offers a series of profound reflections on the meaning of the
Mass. For the words of consecration ('This is my body . . .'),
see especially p. 83ff.

Dictionary of Biblical Theology, (ed.) Xavier Leon-Dufour,
(tr.) under direction of P. Joseph Cahill SJ, Geoffrey
Chapman, London 1978.
The entry for *spouse* gives a comprehensive analysis of the
application of this term to God and Christ in the Old and New
Testaments.

The Catechism of the Catholic Church, Geoffrey Chapman,
London, 1994.
§§ 1615–17 outline the relationship between marriage and
Christ's gift of self to the Church.

Notes
1 Personal communication.
2 This sentence refers to Genesis 2:24, where Paul sees a prophesy of the marriage of Christ and the Church. Cf. note to Eph.
  5:31–2 in *The New Jerusalem Bible*.
3 I am assuming some familiarity with the liturgy of the Church.
  If necessary, consult the reading list at the end of this chapter.
4 Jn 19:30.
5 Cf. Mt 26:26-28 and *The Sunday Missal*, Collins Liturgical
  Publications, 1975, pp. 24–5.
6 Gn 1:28; 2:24.
7 This section owes much to a discussion with Ruth Burrows.
8 Song 5:7 and note *f*.
9 Interview in *The Times*, Friday 21 February 1986.
10 Jn 17:13.
11 See chapter two.
12 See chapter six.
13 'General Intercessions for Good Friday', *The Sunday Missal*,
   p. 198.
   For a full discussion of a believer–non-believer marriage, see my
   A Marriage in Our Time.

Chapter Nine

Perseverance and Fidelity

I believe in the sun even when it is not shining.
I believe in love where feeling is not.
I believe in God even if he is silent.
Words discovered on the wall of a cellar where a
victim of Hitler's persecution hid and died.[1]

Can anything cut us off from the love of Christ – can hardships or
distress, or persecution, or lack of food and clothing, or threats or
violence ... No; we come through all these things triumphantly
victorious, by the power of him who loved us.
Romans 8:35 and 37

'Marriages are much more "salvageable" than most people
think', a friend of mine said to me recently. She was talking
about a woman who had come to her for advice and support,
because the husband had fallen in love with another woman
and wanted to set up home with her. This was obviously only
the bare bones of the situation, but my friend's comment
applies more widely than just to this one marriage, which
appeared to be on the rocks.

People, rightly, want much more from marriage now than
a merely practical arrangement, in which the husband brings
in the money and the wife looks after home and children.
People want happiness, love and in short, a good relationship
between husband and wife. When this does not happen immediately, or if things begin to go wrong, there is a tendency to
discard the 'old' relationship and seek happiness with a new

partner. In a society which expects everything on a plate, marriage partners often expect happiness on a plate too. But is this the whole story? Is happiness the last word? Is marriage (even a difficult marriage) not, as Christians believe, anchored in Christ?

Being Happy and Being Blessed

Just before distributing communion at Mass, a Catholic priest holds up the consecrated elements, saying 'This is the Lamb of God – Happy are those who are called to his supper . . .' At this point many priests substitute *blessed* for *happy*, because we are not always happy, but we are always *blessed* – no matter how we feel.[2] The word *blessed* refers to how things *are*, rather than how they *feel*. Christ's gift of self to us is always, objectively, a blessing, whether we feel happy, subjectively, or not.

In the same way, the mutual gift of husband and wife, through vows and consummation, always create a marriage, which exists in itself, objectively, no matter how the spouses may (come to) feel about it, subjectively. The husband who has fallen in love elsewhere may *feel* that he is no longer bound to his wife, but the marriage (if valid[3]) still exists and may yet be rescued with the good will of both parties.[4]

However, fewer people are prepared to put up with a less than ideal marriage, as the increasing frequency of divorce shows. For many couples the continued existence of the marriage depends on how they feel about it, which places a question mark over the whole marriage. The spouses have married not 'for better for worse, till death do us part', but 'as long as we are happy together'. Such an attitude, even if subconscious, is likely to put the marriage under stress from the beginning, so that any serious difficulty may prompt one or both partners to ask, 'Is it worth persevering?' On the other hand, if the couple start from the basis that they are committed for life and that the marriage is an objective reality, then they are much more likely to succeed.

Relating to What Is

The Marriage Exists

A recent church document states that once a man and a woman have chosen each other with '*equal* freedom', and have married,

> they establish a personal state in which love becomes something that is owed, entailing effects of a juridical nature as well.[5]

What does this legalistic language, used by Pope John Paul II in an address to a group of Canon lawyers, mean? It means that once the marriage exists, one could almost say as an independent entity, then husband and wife owe each other everything, because they have created a 'partnership of the whole of life', a partnership in which they have promised to love each other as Christ loves the Church.[6]

Loving someone does not necessarily mean *feeling* love towards him or her, though often, of course, the two go together. Loving a person means *acting* lovingly towards that person. In the final analysis, this means desiring everything that is good for the other[7] and, in a marriage, it means honouring[8] the other with all that is due to him or her.

In his book *School for Prayer* the Orthodox Archbishop Anthony Bloom has given a good example of the difference between loving and *feeling* love. The Archbishop imagines a man returning from the fields, dead beat after a long day's work. If at that moment, the Archbishop says, his wife were to ask him, 'Do you love me?' the truthful answer would be 'yes'. In terms of his fundamental attitude to his wife and his commitment to her, he does love her. If she were to press the question, the Archbishop goes on, and ask 'do you really feel love for me at this moment?' then the answer would have to be, 'No, at the moment I don't feel anything except my aching back!' It is, of course most unlikely that any wife would ask such questions at such a time, but the Archbishop is making a point which is that,

... underneath all the exhaustion, there is a live current of love.[9]

The story would, of course, be equally true, if it was the wife who was shattered and the husband asking the questions. In both cases it is the objective reality of the marriage that matters, rather than what they feel at the time.

Situations of this kind occur in every marriage and it is the will to reach beyond them that can make the difference between a marriage holding together and falling apart. Husband and wife can only 'will the marriage', if they believe that it is truly for life, so that their love becomes an act of faith too.

The Will to Love

One of the clearest examples I have found of a love which at any rate begins as an act of will appears in Susan Howatch's novel *Ultimate Prizes*. The main character is an Anglican Archdeacon, Stephen, who works in a small cathedral city somewhere in England. Stephen is a widower who feels strongly attracted to a 'society' girl, much younger than himself. They eventually marry, with very mixed motives on both sides, and the marriage turns out to be, in human terms, a disaster. He realises that he has never really loved her, and her phobia of sexual intercourse and childbirth threaten to make the marriage impossible from the very beginning. He is an intellectual, she is a socialite, they come from different backgrounds and the child that might have brought them closer together is stillborn. But out of this impossible scenario are born both his realisation that she has come to love him and his decision to love her in return and remain faithful to her.

While Dido, the wife, is in hospital after the baby's death, Stephen seeks advice from a fellow clergyman, saying that he cannot see a way of continuing his marriage, he cannot even go and visit his wife and listen to her 'prattle' that evening. The reply he gets is tough and uncompromising,

What ... is the hidden message which your wife is so franti-
cally trying to convey to you amidst the torrents of self-centred
monologue? ... have you ever made any profound attempt to
understand why she's the way she is? ... Exert your very
considerable willpower, give the appropriate instructions to
your ox-like constitution and get over to that hospital to minis-
ter to this stranger who so desperately wants to communicate
with you.[10]

In obedience he goes to visit his wife and is indeed attentive
and loving to her. To his great surprise he is able to say (as
he later tells it),

'My dearest Dido!' I exclaimed, and although in one sense I
was acting, in another sense – the only sense that mattered ...
– I was painfully sincere. 'What must you be thinking of me?
I'm sure you're feeling utterly deserted!'[11]

He now knows that all that is required of him is the will to
love her and already he feels that he has been given the
strength to do so. The visit is a turning point in their lives and
for the first time they actually talk to each other about some
of their difficulties and begin to resolve them.
    When he speaks to his priest-counsellor again that evening,
Stephen says,

All that matters ... is that I've been shown the way to survive
my marriage... a miracle ...which is more than I deserve.[12]

And, later still, when he is home at last, and sits down to
write a response to Dido's letter expressing her love for him
(left with him before she went into hospital), Stephen is able
to reflect that with love all things are possible – even a happy
marriage between apparently ill-matched partners

Picking up my pen to answer Dido's letter ... I thought no
more of failure and misery, but began to write my Christian
message of hope in the most loving terms I could devise.[13]

Stephen and Dido have been given the will to love and that is
what makes their 'impossible' marriage possible.

Marriage and Prayer: When We Feel Nothing

The difficulties of this marriage are perhaps unusual, but there are times in every marriage when one or both partners do not feel very loving towards the other. This lack of feeling happens in our relationship with God too, and I think it is helpful to compare the two situations, both of which concern the expression of a love that we know is there, but cannot feel.

Dryness in Prayer – and in Marriage

Prayer is time spent exclusively focused on God. It is like time alone with one's husband or wife, it is a time for intimacy in word and action, a time when we expect to feel something! Yet, as far as prayer is concerned, it is a common experience to seek this intimacy with God, and feel nothing. It is often referred to as 'dryness' in prayer and it is a time when our faith and love for God are tested, when our will to persevere is all that binds us to God (from our side). Anyone who has seriously tried to pray will say that the time when we feel nothing is the time to persevere. The same is true of a human relationship and of marriage in particular. The thing to focus on is the objective reality: I have given myself unconditionally to this man or woman, our marriage is a reality and, if all else fails, this is what I must hold on to.

Sr Wendy Beckett speaks of the importance of relying on the grace of the Mass and the Sacraments, which is there for us to 'tap into', no matter how we *feel*.[14] Just as the Mass is an objective reality, so marriage is such a reality. I can believe, even if I cannot feel, that this marriage exists, that I love him and he loves me with a love that is like the love between Christ and the Church. When a marriage is in apparently insurmountable difficulties, this is the reality that will sustain it.

Frailty

Marriage is an image of the Christ-Church relationship, but just as there are many broken and frail people in the Church, so marriages are made between people who are not perfect and who are constantly in need of God's help to overcome their frailty. It is one of the teachings of the Church that the sum of frailty and sinfulness within her will never be so great that she ceases to be the Church and the Holy Spirit leaves her.[15] The Christ-Church 'marriage' cannot be dissolved nor can a valid, sacramental and consummated marriage be dissolved, as it is kept in existence by the fidelity of Christ to the Church. His fidelity underpins the commitment of the spouses and keeps them together as long as *both* let themselves be supported by him, whether consciously or, in cases where only one spouse believes, by seeking to do all that is right.

What effect does the frailty and brokenness of its members have on the Church, on the one hand, and on individual marriages, on the other? Is there a difference between the two cases? Yes, I think there is. Even if some church members behave badly, there will always be others, sometimes only a few, who remain faithful to Christ and who can therefore project an unsullied image of the Church. On the other hand, if both partners in a marriage stop behaving as married people, their marriage can no longer be seen as a complete witness to Christ's fidelity to the Church. In such a case the mutual gift has been given, the marriage exists and the spouses are bound to each other, but for the time being at least, there is no interaction between them, no fruit, and their witness to Christian fidelity is obscured.

Perfection, both in the Church as a whole and in individual Christians, and hence individual marriages, will come only when everyone has let their love be shaped by Christ. In the Christ-Church marriage one partner, Christ, already loves perfectly, whereas the other is moving towards greater fidelity. In a sense Christ loves in both. In an ordinary human marriage both partners are learning to love perfectly by letting Christ love in them, which is a long, slow process. Where, in all this, is the springtime of love, the falling in love and the delight in each other?

Love and Emotion

The Song of Songs which we have looked at earlier[16] describes in moving terms the deep longing and strong feelings between the *Lover* who says,

> *I come into my garden ...*
> *my promised bride ...*
> *I eat my honey and my honeycomb ...*[17]

To which the *Beloved* replies,

> *Awake, north wind ...*
> *Breathe over my garden ...*
> *Let my love come into his garden ...*[18]

One could say that this book of the Bible gives a picture of the springtime of love, certainly of the 'falling in love' and of the consummation. These 'springtime' feelings of the courtship and marriage can and do recur throughout the marriage and their recurrence with ever deeper meaning can inspire anew the commitment made in youth.

However, this way of loving and being in love is not the whole story of any marriage and there is another, less well known, book of the Bible which shows a different side to marriage. The Book of Tobit, probably written about 200 BC[19] (a couple of hundred years later than the presumed date of the Song of Songs), sets out to edify the reader through a story showing God's providence in action. In this case his providence leads to the meeting of Sarah and Tobias and their eventual marriage, which is described as willed by God from the beginning.[20]

The cultural setting for the story is one in which it was considered a duty and a right to marry within the clan. As Sarah is Tobias' kinswoman, he, according to patriarchal custom, has the right to marry her. We hear how Tobias' father Tobit sends him to Sarah's father, with whom they have had no contact for many years. Tobias claims his right to marry Sarah, to which her father agrees, saying that before they lie down for the night, they must pray together. (The marriage takes place against a background of considerable tension, as Sarah had been given in marriage seven times before, but every time the bridegroom has been killed by a demon before the marriage could be consummated.[21])

I do not think this story should be taken literally, rather it is meant to teach us about the good that comes from doing God's will, in this case doing what is right according to the customs of the time.

Sarah and Tobias do indeed pray before lying down for the night and their prayer speaks of married love not so much in terms of passionate longing and physical arousal as of doing what is right. Their words point to the commitment of the will that is at the heart of every lasting love and their prayer for a long life together is heard:

You are blessed, O God of our fathers;
blessed too is your name
for ever and ever ...

You it was who created Adam,
you who created Eve his wife
to be his help and support;
and from these two the human race was born.
You it was who said,
'It is not right that the man should be alone;
let us make him a helper like him.'

And so I take my sister [kinswoman][22]
not for any lustful motive,
but I do it in singleness of heart.
Be kind enough to have pity on her and on me
and bring us to old age together.
And together they said, 'Amen, Amen', and lay down for the
*   night.*[23]

In spite of the emphasis on the commitment of the will, one cannot imagine that the two young people did not also have feelings for each other like the ones described in the Songs of Songs, just as there are hints in the Song of Songs of the lovers' willingness to suffer for each other, together with an awareness that their marriage will not be entirely a bed of roses.[24]

These two books of the Bible do not contradict but rather complement each other. Without the Song of Songs we get an altogether too solemn impression of the dignities and duties of marriage, but without Tobit we might be tempted to overemphasise the erotic aspect of marriage.[25]

Will and Emotion

The will and the emotions are not mutually exclusive, rather, one could say that the emotions put flesh on the will, but the will gives structure to our decisions and ensures that we stick to them in times of trial. To love is to seek the true good and hence the true happiness of the beloved. If we do that, then happiness and blessedness come together, because when we know ourselves to be blessed, then we are also, fundamentally, happy.[26] What I am and what I feel come together.

Final Reflections

Nothing can dissolve a valid marriage, but it takes the unwavering commitment of both partners, as well as their openness to grace, to stay in the marriage 'till death do us part'. As already mentioned, it is surprising how salvageable marriages can be. Nevertheless, there are cases where it seems that no amount of perseverance and fidelity, on the part of one spouse at least, can save the marriage. What of the gift then? The next chapter will consider this painful reality.

Summary

This chapter draws a parallel between our relationship with God and with our marriage partners. In both cases we can experience times of 'feeling nothing' or of 'dryness'. In these situations contemporary society encourages us to give up on a relationship rather than to persevere. The chapter shows that feelings are important, but are not the ultimate basis of love.

Further Reading

John Paul II, *The Theology of the Body*, pp. 368–77.
These pages contain detailed reflections on the interpretation of The Song of Songs and The Book of Tobit of the Bible.

Susan Howatch, *Ultimate Prizes*, Collins, London, 1989.
A novel describing, from an Anglican point of view, the potential of fidelity and perseverance in a particularly unpromising marriage. See pp. 417–77 in particular.

Notes

1 Quoted by Terry Waite in *Taken on Trust*, Hodder and Stoughton, London, Sydney, Auckland 1993, p. 358.
2 *The Sunday Missal*, p. 50.
3 See chapter ten.
4 *Catechism of the Catholic Church*, §1640.
5 John Paul II, Discourse to the Tribunal of the Roman Rota, 21 January 1999. My emphasis. See also 'Family, Marriage and *de facto* Unions', § 21, *in Briefing*, 13 December 2000, p. 32.
6 *Catechism of the Catholic Church*, §1601ff. and chapters five to eight of this book.
7 Karol Wojtyla (Pope John Paul II), *Love and Responsibility*, p. 138. First published in Polish 1960.
8 See chapter seven.
9 Archbishop Anthony Bloom, *School for Prayer*, Libra Books, Darton Longman & Todd, London 1971, p. 28.
10 Susan Howatch, *Ultimate Prizes*, Collins, London, 1989, pp. 458–9.
11 Ibid., p. 460.
12 Ibid., p. 469.
13 Ibid., pp. 476–7.
14 'Simple Prayer' in *Clergy Review* February 1978, as reprinted in Ruth Burrows, *Ascent to Love,* The spiritual Teaching of St John of the Cross, Sheed & Ward, London 2000, Dimension Books Inc., Starucca 1992, p. 68.
15 *Catechism of the Catholic Church*, §§ 823 and 830.
16 See chapter six.
17 Sg 5:1.
18 Sg 4:16.

19 *The New Jerusalem Bible*, 'Introduction to Tobit, Judith and Esther', pp. 621ff., esp. pp. 622 and 623.

20 Tobit 6:18.

21 Tobit 3:8.

22 Since the marriage takes place because Sarah and Tobias are related, I think this is the likely meaning of 'sister' here, (cf. Tobit 6:18) rather than 'bride', as in Song 4:9.

23 Book of Tobit 8:5–9.

24 See chapter six.

25 For a discussion of further aspects of the Book of Tobit, see John Paul II, *The Theology of the Body*, pp. 375–7.

26 Karol Wojtyla (Pope John Paul II), *Love and Responsibility*, p. 138.

Chapter Ten

When the Gift is Rejected

Being rooted in the personal and total self-giving of the couple, and being required by the good of the children, the indissolubility of marriage finds its ultimate truth [in God's plan] . . .as a fruit, a sign and requirement of the absolutely faithful love that God has for man and the Lord Jesus has for the Church.

Pope John Paul II[1]

In particular we need to give a new start to those families which have been broken and grievously wounded through separation or divorce. For these especially we must all have the greatest love, respect, gentleness and compassion. These are our brothers and sisters, deeply wounded and suffering. Let no one judge them. Welcome them within the community of the Church and help them to experience the life-giving love and compassion which will in time lead to healing and new life.

Archbishop Peter Smith[2]

Not so long ago I went to a funeral Mass in a Catholic Church. The wife had died and the grieving husband and children were in the congregation along with friends and acquaintances. This sounds like any funeral, any time in the Church's history, but this funeral was particularly 'of our time'. Husband and wife had been separated for some years, so he was grieving, yes, but in a complicated and perhaps particularly painful way. Neither spouse had remarried, so their separate and solitary existences represented one way of carrying on with life after a marriage breakdown. As I looked round, I saw a number of couples who were still, as far as I knew, happily married after many years, but I also realised that the mourning husband was not the only one in a difficult marital situation.

At either end of my pew were a (Catholic) husband and wife, divorced and now married to other people, one of them accompanied by the new partner. It was as if I was surrounded by the whole spectrum of what can happen to a marriage, both for good and for ill, but with the sad image of marriage breakdown in the foreground.

What Marriage is: a Reminder

This is a good time to remind ourselves of the meaning of marriage as a lifelong and faithful mutual gift of self of a man and a woman.

The Will to Give

In Christian marriage the mutual consent and gift are like that of Christ to the Church, as we have seen in chapter eight. The spouses commit themselves to each other in total fidelity, while both live, and Christ offers them the strength to make the seemingly impossible promise of staying together for life. Yet the lived reality of marriage is often far from ideal and this is where the temptation to give up can make itself felt. We saw this in the previous chapter, in the case of Dido and Stephen, who were anything but well matched, but who nevertheless decided to remain in and work at their marriage.

Among my own Christian contemporaries I know of a wife who took her husband back after he had moved out of the home to have an affair. He was not particularly sorry for what he had done, but the new 'love' had tired of him. 'So why did you let him come back?' I asked the wife. 'I'm committed to him,' she said, 'he's my husband and nothing can change that.' She now treats him as lovingly as if the whole episode had never happened.

The wife's words put in a nutshell what a German author

has expressed in particularly clear theological language:

> Sacramental [that is, Christian] marriage is wholly structured according to the Christ-Church relationship. Nothing can ever disrupt this relationship: the love of Christ for the Church and the Church for Christ will never end. The human relationship structured according to this same pattern – the dedication of Christ to the Church and the Church's loving response – shares the same permanence ... if marriage were allowed to come to an end with the loss of love on the part of the spouses, it would become detached from its sacramental moorings only to drift in the sea of subjectivism and individualism ... Hence, fundamental as mutual love is to contracting a marriage worthy of the human person – and, indeed, to married life itself – the partners are nonetheless deprived of the power to dispose of the marriage itself. *The solidarity of marriage is distinct from that of every other human encounter based on love; for other encounters bring into existence a kind of community which actually comes to an end if love dies; but when two people contract a marriage they enter into a community whose essence they have not created but which has been predetermined by God through Jesus Christ.*[3]

My friend had decided to live according to the fundamental meaning and commitment of her Christian marriage, whatever the cost.

Content to Stay together

In times when there is a general expectation of instant success, in relationships too, it is easy to forget that happy marriages do not drop out of the sky. Marriages (like people!) can grow and develop, so that a good marriage can result from very modest beginnings.

The document on *The Christian Family in the Modern World (Familiaris Consortio)* speaks of not making excessive demands on the faith of couples intending to marry:

> As for wishing to lay down ... criteria that would concern the level of faith of those to be married, this would above all

involve grave risks. In the first place, the risk of making unfounded and discriminatory judgments; secondly, the risk of causing doubts about the validity of marriages already celebrated, with grave harm to Christian communities, and new and unjustified anxieties to the consciences of married couples.[4]

As long as the couple wish to and are committed to give the marriage a chance, it usually has a chance, however unpromising it may look at the beginning. It is when things go wrong that people sometimes begin to look for 'ways out', which, in our society, often means separation and divorce and Christians are not immune to this trend.[5] Of the possible solutions to serious marital difficulties a temporary separation is the one that can most readily be reversed.

Separating for a Time

A temporary separation may be helpful in cases such as the repeated breaking of promises, persistent infidelity or the addiction to alcohol or drugs of one partner. In such situations it may be necessary to separate for the sake of the 'other' partner and any children of the marriage and the Church recognises that such a need can arise.[6] (I am, of course, not speaking of cases where husband and wife have to live apart for a while for practical reasons, such as job or study demands).

Since mutual trust is one of the 'foundation stones' of marriage, it can become impossible to live with someone who regularly breaks his or her promises. This was the case with an actor who had promised his wife, many times, not to accept work that kept them apart for too long, but kept taking on 'just one more job', that would do precisely that. One day he came home after yet another 'long job', to find their flat empty; his wife had decided to give him an object lesson on what he was doing to their marriage. The shock brought it home to him that he could not have a marriage *and* be away for so much of the time. It took a long time to heal their marriage, but the wife did eventually move back, and this time the husband kept his promise not to accept any more 'long term' jobs away. In this case the temporary separation became a stepping stone towards the healing of the marriage and thus confirmed the hope expressed in the document on the *Christian Family in the Modern World*, that separated spouses might be able to return to married life.[7]

Catholics and Marriage Breakdown

There is a general assumption among Catholics that the Church cannot dissolve any marriage. It would be more accurate to say that, once it has been consummated, the Church cannot dissolve a valid sacramental marriage, that is, a marriage between two baptised Christians. However, the situation is different if one partner is not baptised and the marriage therefore is not a sacrament.

The Full Reality

Speaking of marriages between two unbaptised persons, one of whom has become a Christian, St Paul says that if the unbeliever wishes to depart, then let him or her depart and the Christian is not bound to the marriage. However, it is important to stress that St Paul urges the new convert to do all he or she can to live in peace with the non-believer:

> As a wife, how can you tell whether you are to be the salvation of your husband; as a husband, how can you tell whether you are to be the salvation of your wife?[8]

It is only if the non-believer fights the faith of the believer or departs because of it that the new Christian is free to enter another marriage. (This is known as the 'Pauline Privilege').[9] The possibility of dissolving a non-sacramental bond in favour of the faith, as in the case envisaged by St Paul, has been further widened by the Church to include other types of non-sacramental marriages, whether between two unbaptised people or between an unbaptised man or woman and a baptised Christian. In the latter case, only the pope, as Peter's successor, can make the decision to dissolve the bond, (therefore known as the 'Petrine Privilege').[10]

It may seem strange that only some marriages are indissoluble, but, as we have seen earlier, it is the sacrament, the commitment like that of Christ to the Church, that makes the marriage indissoluble. I would go further and say that, just as a marriage is only 'constituted in its full reality'[11] when it has been consummated, in a similar way, it has only reached its full reality, when it has become an image of Christ's fidelity to the Church, in the sacrament of matrimony. It is when such a marriage breaks down that Catholics, and sometimes other Christians, experience the greatest difficulty and this is the situation I want to consider in the following sections.

Catholics and Divorce

The social stigma that used to attach to marriage breakdown and divorce has almost gone from our generation, but it lives on in the mistaken belief that divorce in itself is a serious sin, so that a divorced Catholic is always excluded from communion. An American priest, whose parents were divorced, told me that his mother stayed away from Mass for years after her marriage breakdown, because she genuinely believed that she could no longer receive the Eucharist, and found it too painful to go to Mass without communion. This is a widespread misunderstanding, both inside and outside the Church, which causes much unnecessary suffering to people who are already suffering enough.

On the other hand, civil divorce does not affect the status of the marriage as far as the Church is concerned, since the partners are still considered to be married. A Catholic in this situation finds him or her self bound to a spouse they are no longer living with and seemingly without any realistic prospect of healing the marriage. How do people react in such cases? There are three basic possibilities, remaining faithful to the 'broken' marriage, entering into a new marriage outside the Church, or applying for a declaration of nullity and I will consider each of these possibilities in turn.

Faithful to the Marriage

The promise to remain faithful 'till death do us part' comes at a high price, because even if the spouses have to separate or one spouse is unfaithful, this does not invalidate the promise. In this situation the temptation to find a new partner is great, but there are nevertheless people who remain faithful to the marriage in spite of the loneliness and the difficulty of bringing up any children alone. A friend of mine, now long dead, found herself abandoned by her husband in favour of another woman. Left with several children to raise, she nevertheless carried on alone, faithful to a husband who had rejected her gift of self and, at any rate, attempted to revoke his own gift.

There can be a kind of joy, if not happiness, in being true to a marriage partner who has left the home, and such a fidelity is surely also a constant invitation to the other spouse to remember his or her gift and return. When one spouse remains faithful, though all outward signs of the marriage have been destroyed, it is a sign not only that Christ is faithful, but of trust in his help, when all else seems to have failed. It is this kind of fidelity that Pope John Paul II spoke of when he said:

> It is ... proper to recognise the value of the witness of ... abandoned spouses ... who ... have not entered a new union: these spouses too give an authentic witness to fidelity, of which the world today has great need. For this reason they must be encouraged and helped by the pastors and the faithful of the Church.[12]

When the deserted partner remains faithful to the marriage, the assumption must, of course, be that he or she believes the marriage to be a valid one.

A New Marriage outside the Church

Sometimes it seems too hard to go through life alone, so many Catholics enter a second, non-Catholic, marriage after a civil divorce.

I once knew a man, whose wife left him after many years of marriage. He had been a practising Catholic all his life, very much wanted to remain faithful to the teaching of the Church, but found it impossible to be alone. After the divorce he remarried outside the Church, though he knew that, from the Church's point of view, he was still bound to his first wife.

Some marriages break down after only a short time together. I once met a young Scandinavian man (a Catholic) who had married a beautiful Portuguese girl. After a few months of marriage, she went home to 'Mum', for good, because she had found the difference in culture too difficult to cope with. After some years the husband, going out of his mind with loneliness, began to look for another companion. I do not know what happened, but the prospect of a man in his late twenties facing his whole life alone is bleak, as indeed is that of a young woman in a Catholic country, with a 'failed' marriage behind her.

Why did these people not at least look into the possibility of a declaration of nullity, that is, a declaration that the first marriage was not a marriage in the eyes of the Church? After all, if granted, such a declaration would have them free to marry in a Catholic Church. There are many reasons why people do not investigate this possibility, but I think the main ones are that they do not know and are afraid to ask what this technical term means, and even if they do know, they may not feel able to face the necessary legal procedure with the inevitable reliving of old, painful memories. However, a new marriage without such a declaration has serious consequences for their lives within the Church.

Effects of a New Marriage outside the Church

Since Christian marriage is for life, a Catholic cannot remarry in the Catholic Church during the lifetime of the spouse. Those who do remarry remain members of the Church, but are unable to share fully in the Eucharist by receiving communion.[13] Remarriage after divorce therefore has more serious consequences for Catholics than for most other people and I will return to this question in chapter eleven.

Seeking a Declaration of Nullity

In order to be called a Christian marriage a marriage has to reflect the Christ-Church marriage in essentials, but there are situations where what looked like a Christian marriage may not have been such a marriage after all. If one of the spouses has any doubt on this point, the Church authorities can review the marriage and, if the doubts are confirmed, it can make a declaration of nullity.

Such a declaration does not mean that there was 'nothing', nor does it take away the pain of the breakdown of a human relationship, which the partners may once have thought was for life. But it does enable them to begin again and to give the gift of self with the fullness of meaning that it has in a Christian marriage. I cannot help feeling that much heartache could be avoided if, where appropriate, people sought a declaration of nullity within a reasonable time scale of the marriage breakdown, so that they would know where they stood, before getting involved with someone else.[14]

What Does Nullity Mean?

The idea of nullity is not easy to understand, even for Catholics, so I did what I often do, when I want to clarify an issue, I talked to my husband who is a computer scientist. 'The way you have described the Church's review of a marriage in the context of a nullity case sounds very much like a process called "pattern matching" in computer science,' he said. 'This involves comparing two files, to see if they are identical or not. In order to be called identical, the two files have to agree on all essential points.' 'I think something similar happens in a nullity case,' he added.

After listening to this analogy, it struck me that the Catholic Church's concept of Christian marriage could be seen as a circle, which had to contain certain essential elements, such as free consent, lifelong commitment, fruitfulness and Christ-like mutual love, in order to be considered a Christian marriage by the Church. The marriage in question could also be described as a circle containing all or only some of these elements.

Therefore, when deciding whether a given marriage corresponds to its understanding of the term, the Church carries out a process of 'pattern matching'. It compares its own circle with that of the marriage in question to see how closely they match and if the marriage lacks essential elements, the Church may be able to make a declaration of nullity.[15]

There is a further similarity between the results of the pattern matching in computer science and the nullity procedure. In both cases the result of the investigation has to be either yes or no. The two files are either identical or not, the marriage is either a Christian, sacramental marriage, or it is not.

However, the whole concept of nullity is alien to many people, who see it simply as 'divorce Catholic style', but since lifelong fidelity to marriage vows is at the very heart of the Church's teaching, there has to be a way of determining, in cases of doubt, whether a man and woman are in fact married, or not. What happens in practice in such cases?

The Tribunal

Every Catholic diocese has a so-called 'tribunal' staffed by canon (church) lawyers and with lay 'auditors' who gather evidence for the cases before them. The task and ministry of the tribunal is to determine whether an individual marriage has all the essential elements necessary for a Christian marriage.

There are, for instance, cases where the partners did not give free consent to the marriage. Or one of them did not know what marriage was, and so made his or her vows on the wrong assumptions. Perhaps one partner was suffering from a form of mental illness, which prevented him or her from fully appreciating the extent of the commitment. Or perhaps one or both was unable to assume the task of married life, for instance due to financial irresponsibility. In cases like these the marriage never contained all the elements necessary for a Christian marriage. An annulment can then be part of a healing process, 'like the Twelve Steps', as one member of the Association of Separated and Divorced Catholics put it[16] and an increasing number of annulments are granted each year, both in Britain and worldwide.[17]

In spite of that, the word 'tribunal' still has overtones of 'Spanish Inquisition' for many people, including Catholics. Only recently I spoke to someone who had been through an annulment process some twenty years ago. The process resulted in her being set free from a marriage entered into on false premises, but in spite of that, and a happy subsequent marriage, she said that she probably would not have begun the process, had she known what would be involved. I think things have got better since then. Certainly the reality, from what I have seen of it, could not be more different. I have deliberately used the term 'ministry' about the work of the tribunal, because that is how many canon lawyers, including those I have met, see it.[18] Very often, in such cases, it is a matter of helping to release people from what they thought was a 'dead-end' situation.

A Grey Area

Some of the examples mentioned above are more obvious than others, so that one could speak of a sliding scale, at one end of which is the perfect match between the Church's understanding of marriage and an individual marriage. At the other end of the scale is a circle so 'un-matching' that there can be no doubt that this was never a marriage – for instance if there is coercion.

These are the extremes of the scale, but there is an area in the middle, a grey area, where different tribunals could, in good faith, make different interpretations of the 'match'. Fr Timothy Buckley quotes a case in which a young woman petitioned for an annulment on the grounds that she went ahead with her (now broken) marriage in spite of serious doubts at the time of the wedding. Her anxiety had been such that she had made a verbal pact with her fiancé that they would get a divorce if the marriage did not work out. However, when the marriage did break down, the husband attributed this to the fact that his wife had met another man, whom she now wanted to marry. The wife consistently denied this as a reason for the breakdown, but since there was no independent evidence for the 'pact' with her (then) fiancé, this weakened her case for *an intention against the permanence of marriage*, which could have made a declaration of nullity possible. Both the original tribunal and the one she appealed to, felt that it could not be certain that the 'other man' had not been a contributory factor in the breakdown of the marriage. Because the tribunal has to assume that a marriage is valid in canon law, unless there is clear evidence to the contrary, the declaration of nullity was not granted.[19]

This is the kind of situation in which, given slightly different circumstances, (for instance a more communicative bride or a more observant family), a declaration of nullity might conceivably have been granted. It is also the kind of case that can provoke complaints about an 'unfair' system, because a line has to be drawn, a decision has to be made either to grant or not to grant nullity, with consequences that may affect the people concerned for the rest of their lives.

It would be beyond the scope of this book to attempt an evaluation of the present system of tribunals, but it is worth quoting the words of Archbishop Peter Smith with regard to the whole situation of the divorced and remarried:

> I think pastorally, as a priest, that one of the big difficulties is this question of people . . . whose marriages have broken down. They have remarried, in inverted commas, and they cannot or do not feel they are fully part of the Church. They cannot participate in the Eucharist and Penance as they would wish. I would love to see that resolved, but . . . it is not a thing that is going to be easily resolved or very quickly . . . In the meantime I think we have got to be very sensitive to those who are in those . . . situations; and to really convince them . . . [that] they are . . . part of the Church.[20]

The Gift in a Second Marriage after Divorce

What meaning can the gift of self have in an irregular marriage? The gift contradicts the essence of Christian marriage, which is to express the fidelity of Christ. One or both of the partners is married to someone else, and yet, to the couple, the new relationship may appear more meaningful and loving than the one they have left. From a purely subjective point of view, it may even *be* more loving and considerate. The new relationship may have some of the elements of the Church's marriage circle, but the essential likeness to Christ's faithfulness is missing. The act of love in this case expresses what they feel for each other, but it falls short of the mutual gift between Christian spouses, which corresponds to Christ's gift to the Church. These are circumstances from which there is not always an easy way out and which therefore call for the compassion of the whole Church.

The Couples in the Pew

As my thoughts return to the grieving husband and the couples around me at the funeral, and as I think of fellow parishioners in difficult marital situations, I realise that, precisely because the gift of self in marriage is so complete, its rejection is the most profound sorrow anyone can experience. Living with such sorrow for the rest of one's life after a marriage breakdown is the dark side, and the risk, of the total gift of self. It is no wonder that such deeply wounded people sometimes seek healing in the love and acceptance of a new spouse.

If the Church considers that one or both partners is still validly married to someone else, and they want to remain in the Church, then theirs is a hard case indeed. The difficulties of the increasing number of people in this situation is constantly under debate both inside and outside the Church and is, in the words of one Scandinavian bishop, a question that 'simply won't go away'.[21] It is a question which I will consider in the next chapter.

Summary

Situations where the gift of self seems to have been revoked, rejected or emptied of meaning are considered and reactions to marriage breakdown and divorce in a Roman Catholic context are discussed. The concept of nullity and the Church's system of marriage tribunals are explained and the chapter also considers the meaning of the act of love in an 'irregular' marriage.

Further Reading

Timothy Buckley CSSR, *What Binds Marriage*, Roman Catholic Theology in Practice, Continuum, London and New York, Revised and expanded edition 2002 (first published by Chapman 1997).
Based on a study of marriage breakdown and irregular unions involving Catholics, commissioned by the Catholic Bishops' Conference of England and Wales, 'Committee for Marriage and Family Life'. A thorough and readable academic study, including case histories and questions for discussion.

Fr Stephen Gasche, *Marriage Annulment in the Catholic Church*, Catholic Truth Society, London 1998.
A clear and simple explanation by a canon lawyer.

Sr Victoria Vondenberger, RSM, JCL, *Catholics, Marriage and Divorce*, Real People, Real Questions, St Anthony Messenger Press, Cincinnati, Ohio, 2003.
The author is the current tribunal director and canon lawyer for the Archdiocese of Cincinnati and the book is based on answers given to questions about marriage, divorce and nullity on the http://www.oncecatholic.org/reading.asp web site.

Joanna Trollope, *The Rector's Wife*, Berkley Books, New York 1991.
A perceptive novel which deals with marriage breakdown from an Anglican perspective.

See also **Further Reading** for chapter eleven.

Notes

1 *The Christian Family in the Modern World (Familiaris Consortio)*, Apostolic Exhortation of his Holiness Pope John Paul II, Catholic Truth Society, London 1981, § 20.
2 Pastoral Letter for the Feast of the Holy Family, 1999. Archbishop Peter Smith was then Bishop of East Anglia.
3 Michael Schmaus, *Dogma*, vol. 5, p. 297f., English translation, Sheed and Ward, London, 1975. My emphasis.
4 Pope John Paul II, *Familiaris Consortio*, § 68.
5 Duncan J. Dormor, *The Relationship Revolution: Cohabitaion, Marriage and Divorce in Contemporary Europe*, London: One Plus One, Marriage and Partnership Research, 1992, p. 22; Michael Hornsby-Smith, *Roman Catholics Beliefs in England: Customary Catholicism and Transformations of Religious Authority*, p. 183. (Both references from Timothy Buckley CSSR, *What Binds Marriage*, p. 1.).
6 *Catechism of the Catholic Church*, § 1649.
7 Pope John Paul II, *Familiaris Consortio*, § 83.
8 1 Co 7:16.
9 The marriage with the non-believer is dissolved at the moment the new marriage is entered. See Fr Stephen Gasche, *Marriage Annulment in the Catholic Church*, p. 16f.
10 Fr Stephen Gasche, *Marriage Annulment and the Catholic Church*, p. 16f.
11 See chapter seven.
12 Pope John Paul II, *Familiaris Consortio*, § 20.
13 *Catechism of the Catholic Church*, §1665.
14 A parish priest might be able to throw light on the possibility of nullity or the Diocesan Tribunal can be contacted for information. Contact details of the Tribunal can be found in every Diocesan Handbook or Year Book.
15 Any children born of a marriage declared null are considered legitimate, as the couple believed themselves to be married. See Fr Stephen Gasche, *Marriage Annulment and the Catholic Church*, p. 15.
16 Timothy Buckley CSSR, *What Binds Marriage*, p. 155. The 'Twelve Steps' is a process followed by Alcoholics Anonymous and similar groups.
17 For detailed figures, see Timothy Buckley CSSR, *What Binds Marriage*, p. 152f. According to Buckley, there were just twelve annulments in great Britain in 1968, by 1980 there were nearly

500 such decrees per year in England and Wales and in 1993 (the last year quoted by Buckley) over 1000 affirmative judgements in England and Wales.

18 Ibid., p. 190f.
19 Ibid., p. 74ff.
20 *Catholics and Sex*, transcript of Programme 3 on *Divorce,* London, Compulsive Viewing Limited, 1992, p. 90. Transmitted on Channel Four, 7 December 1992. (My quotation from Timothy Buckley CSSR, *What Binds Marriage*, p. 116f. Archbishop Smith was Rector of Wonersh Seminary at the time.
21 Bishop Czeslaw Kozon, 'Caring for the Divorced and Remarried', *in Katolsk Orientering*, Issue 7, vol. 23, 16 April 1997, p. 5.

Chapter Eleven

Sin and Sexual Sin

You are not your own property ... you have been bought at a
price. So use your body for the glory of God.
1 Corinthians 6:20

'I cannot give them communion, and my heart breaks.'
Catholic priest about divorced and remarried
Catholics in his parish

As we have seen,[1] there has been a tendency among some
church members in the past, to think of sexual pleasure as
inherently sinful and to be tolerated only for the sake of beget-
ting children. This has never been official church teaching,
but many people still think that the Church considers sexual
sin to be worse than any other kind of transgression. This
impression is reinforced by the fact that almost the only
Catholics who are unable to receive communion, on a long
term basis, are those in irregular sexual unions. What is it that
makes sexual sin appear different to any other sin?

Like a Sore Thumb

In the teaching of the Catholic Church serious sin, including
the gift of self outside marriage, requires forgiveness in the
sacrament of reconciliation (confession) before those involved
can rightly go to communion again. However, most of these
can be put right discreetly, and do not lead to a situation
where, Sunday after Sunday, those involved remain in their

seats at communion time, sticking out like sore thumbs.[2] Thus the impression given to the rest of the congregation, and the world outside, is that it is only certain types of sexual sin that exclude from full participation in the life of the Church, namely those that involve an ongoing sexual relationship outside marriage. Many of those living together are unaware of the Church's teaching on this and therefore continue to go to communion, but there is far more awareness of the religious difficulties of divorced Catholics in a second marriage, as we saw in the previous chapter.

Causing Scandal

Over the years I have discussed the question of those in an irregular situation with many different people and often heard comments such as, 'Are these people really committing the most serious sin, as their exclusion from communion seems to indicate? What about the terrible things that sometimes happen in outwardly 'respectable' marriages? It seems a scandal that only this particular group should be excluded.

Our word 'scandal' comes from a Greek word meaning 'stumbling block'. In ordinary everyday language, as used by the people I was speaking to, it means something that troubles people's consciences. In a more technical theological sense, it also means something, which can lead others into sin.[3]

Whenever I have that kind of conversation, I am reminded of a couple I once met at the 'Catholic Dinner' at a British university. They sat opposite me at table and although this is now many years ago, the way she treated him has stayed etched on my mind ever since. She talked incessantly, and quite amusingly, about herself, 'I do this, I do that, as far as I am concerned . . .' Once or twice he made an attempt to say something, which she immediately squashed, not quite saying 'shut up', but her expression said it all. I sat there thinking, 'These people have just been to Mass (the dinner was always preceded by a Mass), they are married, they are supposed to love each other, how can she treat him like that? And why does he let her?' To me it did not look as if they were having an 'off' day, but rather that this was what their marriage was like. I have not met them before or since, so I could have been wrong, but I do not think so. It is the contrast between this kind of 'lived reality' of a marriage and the loving reality of many an 'irregular' union that is troubling to people's consciences.

There is, of course, a difference in that the 'irregular' union is something in itself wrong, which is plain for all to see, whereas the state of any given marriage must always be a matter of opinion and only God knows what is really happening. Here we are up against the contrast between a person's objective state in life (e.g. a married person or a priest) and the subjective way in which he or she lives that state. The fact that one or both partners live their marriage badly does not necessarily mean that it is not a marriage, just as the fact that a priest is not living up to his vocation does not invalidate the Masses he celebrates. In these cases the 'bones' of priesthood or of marriage are there and it may still be possible to clothe them with the 'flesh' of love.

On the other hand, if the Church were to admit those in irregular unions to communion, that could be seen as a scandal in the sense of something leading people into sin and I will return to this question at the end of this chapter.

From Unmarried Union to Marriage

Cohabitation

A recent church document on family, marriage and cohabitation ('*de facto* unions') seeks to present the truth about these in the context of the widespread contemporary tendency to equate cohabitation with marriage. The document explains the Church's teaching about the difference between marriage and cohabitation, while making it clear that its purpose is to differentiate between different ways of forming a household, not to judge those who belong to those households. It is a matter of evaluating actions, not people.[4]

Although there are some overlaps between marriage and cohabitation in terms of emotions and private commitment, there are also important differences. Not every couple 'living together' is committed to a lifelong union, and the relationship is, in any case, a private one, depending heavily on the personal, subjective attitude of the two people involved. On the other hand, marriage is an objective and public commitment and a mutual gift of self of a man and a woman, while both live.[5] As we have seen in chapters eight and nine, there are times in every marriage when it is not primarily the *feeling* of love that holds it together, but the commitment of the will to the existence of this marriage, no matter how the spouses may feel at any given time.[6]

Under the heading *Pastoral Care and Closeness* the document on *de facto* unions refers to Christ's loving and truthful care of everyone he came into contact with as the example for all in the Church to follow. It urges

> Christians . . . to try to understand the personal, social, cultural and ideological reasons for the spread of *de facto* unions.[7]

In 2001, the year after the publication of the document quoted, the bishops of Uruguay made their five-yearly (*Ad Limina*) visit to the Pope to report on their local church. In his address to them Pope John Paul stressed the importance of pastoral care not only for married couples, but also for those in *de facto* unions, who are often considered to be married in Uruguayan society.[8]

In other words, all help and kindness should be shown to people in 'cohabiting' unions, so that, where at all possible, they can make the decision to marry. Thus, in most cases, there is no problem about changing their situation within the Church, so that they can share fully in the Eucharist, if they wish to do so.

Second Marriage after Divorce: Present Solutions

People in a second marriage after divorce are in a far more difficult position, but, for some at least, there are ways of resolving their situation.

New Grounds for Nullity

As mentioned in the previous chapter, there has been a considerable increase in the number of declarations of nullity granted in recent years as well as a fuller understanding on the part of church authorities of what can constitute grounds for nullity. In his book *What Binds Marriage*, Fr Timothy Buckley draws attention to the increase in the number of declarations of nullity now granted on psychological grounds. Until the mid-twentieth century the Church recognised the potentially invalidating effect of mental illness only when it made a responsible act of consent impossible at the time of the marriage.[9] The new Code of Canon Law (1983) includes the following as being 'incapable of contracting marriage':

1. Those who lack sufficient use of reason;
2. those who suffer from a grave lack of discretionary judgement concerning the essential matrimonial rights and obligations to be mutually given and accepted;
3. those who, because of causes of a psychological nature, are unable to assume the essential obligations of marriage.[10]

According to Fr Buckley's survey of diocesan tribunals of England and Wales published in 1997 almost all of the twenty-two dioceses had granted the majority of their declarations of nullity on psychological grounds. Ten estimated that 90% or more were granted on such grounds.[11] The greater understanding of the psychology of human relationships has now made it possible to grant nullity on grounds that would not have been acceptable twenty or thirty years ago.[12]

This deeper understanding of the process by which people decide to marry is a great step forward and a development of the Church's teaching in the sense of 'growth in understanding, knowledge, and wisdom', as we saw in chapter four. However, in the area of the social context in which consent is given there seems to me to be further room for development and I will return to this later in this chapter.

Irregular Unions Involving those already validly Married

Even with a widening range of grounds for nullity, there are some couples who cannot be helped via this avenue. Indeed the very fact that marriage is for life implies the risk of having to live out the vows alone after a spouse has left the home or has become impossible to live with. It cannot simply be assumed that, because, humanly speaking, a marriage has broken down, it was never valid.

For people in this situation, who are in a second union, the only 'official' way back to being able to receive the sacraments is through acknowledging the fact that they are not married in the eyes of the Church and therefore either to separate or cease to share the sexual intimacy of a husband and wife.[13] In my view, this is the only choice which accepts the full consequences of their situation, but this option is so difficult that there is a constant debate within the Church about finding some other way back to the sacraments for people in this predicament.

Action by the Bishops of England and Wales

During the Bishops' Ad Limina visit to the Pope and Roman Congregations in 1997 Cardinal Hume, in his address to the Pope, spoke with compassion about people in irregular unions. He said:

In this century especially, *the relationship between membership of the Church and reception of Holy Communion has been affirmed* and appreciated. It is not surprising that, despite reassurances, those who are not permitted to receive Holy Communion find themselves estranged from the family of the Church gathered for Mass. We are conscious of your deep concern for these couples and their families and your invitation 'to help them experience the charity of Christ ... to trust in God's mercy ... and to find concrete ways of conversion and participation in the life of the community of the Church'. We are anxious to receive encouragement from you to explore every possible avenue by which we may address this important and sensitive aspect of our pastoral ministry.[14]

Since the Scandinavian bishops brought up this question in the same year and were told that the Congregation for the Doctrine of the Faith was considering at least some aspects of the problem, it must be assumed that the Bishops of England and Wales were given a similar response. No specific reference was made to this issue either by Pope John Paul or by Cardinal Murphy-O'Connor during the 2003 *Ad Limina* visit.[15]

Second Marriage after Divorce: Proposed Ways Forward

The 'Orthodox Solution'

One way of resolving the problem, which is often mentioned, is the so-called 'Orthodox solution' to marriage breakdown. In such cases the Orthodox Church, whose sacraments the Catholic Church recognises, offers the possibility of a second marriage, after a period of repentance and penance. Every effort is made to heal the first marriage, but when this is not feasible and a civil divorce has taken place, the Orthodox Church can accommodate a second union within church discipline.

The 'Guidelines for Clergy in the Orthodox Church in America' state that:

> The Orthodox norm for those who marry is one marriage. A second marriage is tolerated under certain circumstances.[16]

The Guidelines go on to say that the fundamental reason for granting permission for a second marriage after divorce is that the people involved consider it necessary for their salvation and that they make a statement to this effect and the local bishop makes the final decision in each case. It is thus clear that Orthodox Christians do not have an automatic right to remarriage after divorce.[17]

There is a penitential aspect to the whole process of entering such a second marriage, as can be seen from the liturgy used only for second marriages, which begins with an appeal for God's mercy and pardon. The rite concludes with St Paul's words about widows remarrying that 'it is better to be married than to be burnt up'[18] as the justification for allowing a second marriage, even after divorce.[19] It is significant that the whole context of the Orthodox approach indicates that these marriages are not seen as sacramental or as images of the total fidelity between Christ and the Church.

While a marriage such as that allowed by the Orthodox Church must be seen as a help towards integrating divorced people who want to remarry, I also think that, theologically, it is a step backwards. In the Gospel of St Mark the Pharisees ask Jesus about the acceptability of divorce, reminding him that Moses allowed them to draw up a 'writ of dismissal'. However, Jesus replies that

> It was because you were so hard hearted that he wrote this command for you. But from the beginning of creation *he made them male and female. This is why a man leaves his father and mother, and the two become one flesh.* They are no longer two, therefore, but one flesh. So then, what God has united, human beings must not divide.

Jesus goes on to say that whoever divorces a wife or husband and marries another is guilty of adultery.[20] Christ's teaching brings marriage back to how it was from the beginning and how, after the coming of Christ, it can be again. Allowing a second marriage after divorce therefore, as far as I can see, means a step back into the Old Testament dispensation, so that I do not think it is an acceptable solution.

A New Phenomenon: The Baptised Non-Believer

The Code of Canon Law states that

> For matrimonial consent to exist, it is necessary that the contracting parties be at least not ignorant of the fact that marriage is a permanent partnership between a man and a woman, ordered to the procreation of children through some form of sexual cooperation.

This ignorance is not presumed after puberty.[21]

The above quotation takes for granted a society in which people in general knew what Christian marriage was, but might not always have known 'the facts of life', so that they might, for instance, have thought that it was possible to get pregnant from kissing. The situation in contemporary society is exactly the opposite, so that there can be few even pre-teenage children who do not know 'the facts of life', but there are many adults, including some who have been baptised, who do not know what Christian marriage is. Undoubtedly most people *want* a marriage to last, but today there is at least the tacit assumption that if it does not work out, they can divorce. As it is the bride and groom who are the ministers of the sacrament of matrimony, it seems to me that, in order to celebrate the sacrament, they must be aware that they are doing so. At the very least, this matter calls for clarification and, not surprisingly, it was one of the questions that the Scandinavian Bishops discussed at their *Ad Limina* visit to the Pope and Roman Congregations in 1997.

Action by the Scandinavian Bishops

The problem had come to the attention of the Scandinavian bishops in connection with marriage breakdown between baptised non-believers. If those involved later wanted to marry a Catholic, this was, at present, impossible, since a marriage between two baptised people (even if non-believers) was automatically considered a sacrament and therefore indissoluble. In an interview after the meeting, the Bishop of Copenhagen argued that, in such cases, one or both partners often did not know what marriage was. Key elements such as lifelong commitment, fidelity and sacramentality were frequently missing from their concept of marriage, so that their original commitment had not been to a marriage as understood by the Church. The Scandinavian bishops, he said, had pleaded for easier access to nullity in such cases and had been told that the matter was already under consideration by the Congregation.[22]

Unofficial Solutions

There are various 'unofficial' solutions to the problems of the divorced and remarried, leading to readmission to communion. For instance, when someone is convinced in conscience that his or her previous marriage was not valid, but this cannot be proved, some priests operate an 'internal forum' solution, based on what those concerned have told him confidentially or in the sacrament of reconciliation. It is clear from research into this subject that practice varies considerably from one priest to another and is wholly dependent on his individual judgement of any given situation.[23] It seems to me that whatever new ways forward may be found have to apply to the whole Church rather than being based on 'ad hoc' solutions used by some clergy and not others.

Prevention Better than Cure

For those not yet married, the way forwards leads through better marriage preparation and also teaching on the significance of marriage for all Catholics, whether they intend to marry or not.

In view of the lack of understanding of what marriage is in society in general, proper preparation for the sacrament, with the necessary time to do so, comes to assume an importance it may not have had in the past. In this light the minimum requirement of six months' notice of the intention to marry, that the father of an impatient young man had thought so excessive, comes to look both reasonable and necessary.[24]

However, I think more could be done in terms of general 'marriage awareness' well before people seriously consider marriage. I was interested to see a suggestion along these lines in a working paper for the Diocesan Synod in Chennai (Madras), India, in 2003. The proposal was that there should be compulsory marriage preparatory classes for all girls aged seventeen and boys aged twenty, irrespective of whether they intended to marry or not. It is not clear how well such a compulsory course would work in a Western[25] setting, but in

my diocese, where young people are confirmed in their mid-
teens, the course material includes a session on the main basic
vocations in life: ordination, the religious life, the single life
and marriage. The vocation of most of the participants will,
of course, be marriage and the course takes this into account.
At the time of writing *Catholic Marriage Care* (UK) is about
to train education workers to speak to school pupils in the
fourteen to sixteen year age group about the meaning of Christian marriage. The young people who have attended such
courses should be better equipped to make an informed decision, once they reach the stage, probably many years later, of
considering marriage seriously.[26]

Reflections on Divorce and Remarriage in the Light of the Christ-Church Marriage

Light on the Image of the Divorced and Remarried

As we have seen, it is possible to compare the teaching of the
Church about marriage to a painting which has not always
been fully lit up. However, in our times, the importance of the
physical gift of self is understood and therefore 'lit up' much
more clearly than it used to be.[27]

In the discussion about communion for the divorced and
remarried who cannot be granted nullity, it seems to me that
the whole focus of attention has been on finding a way to re-
admit them to communion which permits them to continue
living with their new partners. In order to understand the
problem better, I think it is necessary to shift the light to the
picture of the Christ-Church marriage and the sacrament of
matrimony.

Light on the Christ-Church Marriage and the Sacrament of Matrimony

Christian spouses promise to be faithful to each other 'till
death do us part'. This is not only a solemn mutual promise,
sealed by the gift of self, but also a picture of the fidelity of

Christ to the Church. Thus, as we have seen, their marriage is drawn into the Christ-Church relationship and becomes an image of it.[28]

The close connection between the mutual gift in marriage and that of Christ to the Church is expressed clearly in the celebration of the Eucharist. Christ's words of self giving 'This is my Body ...' are true also of the mutual gift between husband and wife 'This is my body ... it is for you.'

Development in Church Teaching about Marriage

Change versus Development

Church authorities are often accused of showing a lack of compassion for people in second, irregular, marriages. 'Why can't it change the rules, so that these people too can have communion?' many lay people ask. 'I cannot give them communion, and my heart breaks', I heard a priest say. The question is whether this is something the Church is able to change.

We saw in chapter four that the question of development in the Faith has been with the Church virtually for as long as it has existed and we saw that development was about clarification and a deeper understanding of the Faith, but not change in fundamental doctrine. It has always been church teaching that there is an inseparable link between Christian marriage and the Christ-Church Marriage.[29] In different ways, both involve a physical gift of self which is exclusive to husband and wife within a commitment of absolute and lifelong fidelity. People who give this gift outside a valid marriage thus contradict the mutual gift that is at the heart of the Eucharist. In my view, church teaching about not receiving communion in those circumstances therefore cannot change, because it would involve changing its fundamental teaching about marriage.

Development

On the other hand, I believe that development can take place in the Church's understanding of the circumstances in which a valid marriage can be entered into. As we have already seen, the reasons for granting a declaration of nullity have been widened to take into account our better understanding of the psychological reasons for a man or woman being unable to take on the responsibilities of marriage. As we have also seen, the Scandinavian bishops have pleaded for easier access to nullity in connection with marriages between baptised non-believers and I believe that there is room for further development in this area. Such development could clearly help a number of people whose first marriages cannot be declared null at present.

In my view, therefore, the way forward for people whose marriages have broken down goes through seeking the truth about the broken marriage. However, even if the grounds for nullity are widened, there will always be cases where a valid marriage has broken down and where one or both spouses are in an irregular union with somebody else. What then?

The Eucharist as Encounter with Christ

In the Gospel accounts those who meet Christ are invited to change through their encounters with him, because he faces them with the truth about themselves, pointing, compassionately, to the sinful aspects of their lives. Christ looks at them with a love that enables them to change, if they want to. As we have seen in the story of the woman caught in adultery, he shows understanding for her situation ('neither do I condemn you'), but he does not condone her sin ('from this moment, sin no more'). In the case of the 'Prodigal Son', as we have also seen, the young man who had lived a life of sexual sin 'came to his senses' and returned to his father.[30] Christ's attitude in these two accounts is the model for our times too, in every difficult situation including that of the divorced and remarried.

For us today, every Eucharistic celebration is an encounter with Christ, comparable to the life-changing encounters in the Gospels. In these loving meetings we see the truth about ourselves, part of which is an awareness of the things that block our way to him. If we are conscious of serious sin, something that keeps us at a distance from Christ, then we need to meet him in the sacrament of reconciliation (confession), before coming close to him in communion. The difficulty for the divorced and remarried is that, in most cases, they want to continue in a situation that objectively contradicts the fidelity of Christ. They therefore cannot receive the sacrament of reconciliation which would open the way to communion.

What is more, part of the truth about their situation is that they have taken on responsibilities which they cannot simply drop in order to 'put matters right' with the Church. They have made a commitment to their partner and to any children they might have, so that the only possible option, at least for the time being, may be to continue living the new partner, while sharing in the aspects of church life that remain open to them.

The Question of Scandal

As mentioned earlier in this chapter, many people feel scandalised or troubled because apparently only those in irregular unions are excluded from communion. I have often heard the point made that being married outside the Church is not the only or the worst sin and this always reminds me of the wife who treated her husband so badly at the Catholic Dinner. No, being in an irregular union is certainly not the only reason for not going to communion. However, it is almost the only situation in which people live publicly in a way which entails ongoing serious sin. That is what keeps them away from communion, not the level of seriousness of their sin, so that there is no real basis for being scandalised about the treatment of these couples. On the other hand, if they were to be allowed to go to communion, it would, as we have seen, be a scandal in the sense of leading people into sin, because it would give the impression that giving the gift of self outside marriage might be compatible with the teaching of Christ.

Conclusion

It has now become clear that sexual sin is not the only unforgivable sin. However, some kinds of sexual sin, those that involve a second marriage after divorce, are more difficult to turn away from than most.

For those in unmarried unions and those whose first marriage can be declared null, there is a comparatively easy way back to sharing fully in the sacraments, by marrying their partners. Those in a marriage outside the Church, but validly married to someone else, are in a more difficult situation, since the way back to communion means ceasing to live as husband and wife and they may not be able to do that.

Are these people then the only ones whose sin, because it is sexual, cannot be forgiven? No, it is not that the sin is sexual, but that those involved, for the time being at least, intend to continue living in a way that blocks their way to the sacraments. However, it is a situation that calls for compassion, not judgement, and for every kindness and help from the local parish, so that they may know that they belong to a church which shares their pain, but cannot deny its own truth.

Part of that truth is that they remain members of the Church and in this capacity there are many things that they can do. They can share in the prayer of the parish community at Mass and also in many other aspects of parish life, such as prayer or Scripture groups. They can also share in the work of Justice and Peace groups, for instance, or that of charitable organisations such as the St Vincent de Paul Society, which gives practical help to the poorest and most disadvantaged people. When they do this, they share in the Church's ministry to all who are in need, an essential ministry in which they can fully participate.[31]

Summary

There are many kinds of sin, sexual sin being only one of them. Unlike most other sins, this can present Catholics (and other Christians) with apparently insoluble problems. This chapter reflects on the difference between sin and sexual sin as it relates to the gift of self in marriage and, particularly, to the reception of communion by those in 'irregular' situations. It also discusses some proposed solutions to this problem. It goes on to show that every encounter with Christ, whether in the Gospels or in the Eucharist, reveals the truth about the person who meets Christ. This truth calls for conversion and a turning away from serious sin. When a couple do not feel able, for the time being at least, to take such conversion to its full conclusion by ceasing to live as husband and wife, they cannot share in Christ's gift of self in the Eucharist. However, the chapter points to the many ways in which, as full members of the Church, they can continue to share in the life of the Church.

Further Reading

Deus Caritas Est, God Is Love, Encyclical Letter of Pope Benedict XVI.
Part II deals with the Church's charitable activity as an essential aspect of its life.

Familiaris Consortio, The Christian Family in the Modern World, Apostolic Exhortation of his Holiness Pope John Paul II.
§§ 79–84 deal with 'Pastoral action in certain irregular situations'.

Cherishing Life, Catholic Bishops' Conference of England and Wales, Catholic Truth Society, London 2004.
§§ 133–6 deal with divorce, nullity and the reception of communion by those in a 'second relationship'.

Kevin T. Kelly, *Divorce & Second Marriage*, Facing the Challenge, New and Expanded Edition, Geoffrey Chapman, London 1996. Discusses pastoral approaches to divorce and remarriage, advocating readmission to communion for some couples in second marriages (p. 77 ff.). Appendix 2 contains a comprehensive selection of official church statements, articles and excerpts from books on divorce and remarriage and the admission to communion of those in irregular unions (pp. 90–236).

See also **Further Reading** for chapter ten.

Notes

1 See chapter four.
2 Canons 915 and 916 of *The Code of Canon Law* state that anyone obstinately persisting in manifestly grave sin or who is conscious of grave sin is not to be admitted to Holy Communion without first having been to sacramental confession. English Translation, Collins Liturgical Publications, London, 1983. See also *Catechism of the Catholic Church*, §§ 2390 and 2350.
3 Most Rev. Dr Anthony Fisher OP, 'Co-Operation in Evil', in Briefing vol. 33. Issue 9, 10 September 2003, p. 28.
4 'Family, Marriage a*nd de facto* Unions', by the *Pontifical Council for the Family*, 21 November 2000. Printed in *Briefing*, vol. 30, Issue 12, 13 December 2000, pp. 22–42. See §§ 12 and 49.
5 Ibid., §§ 9 and 12.
6 Ibid., § 20.
7 Ibid., § 49.
8 http://www.vatican.va Search for 'Uruguay Ad Limina 2001'. Look for 'Address by John Paul II'.
9 Timothy Buckley CSSR, *What Binds Marriage*, pp. 160–3.
10 *The Code of Canon Law*, Can. 1095.
11 Timothy Buckley CSSR, *What Binds Marriage*, p. 161.
12 Ibid.
13 John Paul II, *The Christian Family in the Modern World (Familiaris Consortio)*, § 84 and *Catechism of the Catholic Church*, § 1650.
14 *Briefing*, 27/11 (20 November 1997 : 8 (*sic*)). My emphasis.

15 *Briefing* November 2003, vol. 33, Issue 10, pp. 14–19.

16 'Guidelines for Clergy in the Orthodox Church in America', http://aggreen.net/guidelines/guide04.html#Second and letter from Bishop Tikhon of the Diocese of the West, Orthodox Church of America, posted on the Net at http://www.holy-trinity.org/liturgics/tikhon.second.html. The preference for 'one marriage' is based on the image of the one Christ-Church marriage.

17 *Service Book of the Holy Orthodox-Catholic Apostolic Church*, (tr.) Isabel Florence Hapgood, revised edition with endorsement by Patriarch Tikhon, fourth Edition, Syrian Antiochian Orthodox ARCHDIOCESE OF New York and All North America, New York, 1965, p. 605.

18 1 Co 7:9.

19 'The Stand of the Orthodox Church on Controversial Issues', http://www.goarch.org/print/en/ourfaith/article7101.asp and *Service Book of the Holy Orthodox-Catholic Apostolic Church*, p. 305. See also Timothy Buckley CSSR, *What Binds Marriage*, pp. 172–7.

20 Mk 10:2–12. Passages in italics refer to Gn 2:24.

21 *The Code of Canon Law*, Can. 1096.

22 Interview with Bishop Czeslaw Kozon *in Katolsk Orientering* no. 9, vol. 23, May 1997, p. 7. The report of the Bishops' next *Ad Limina* visit, in 2003, mentioned that marriage and family life were discussed, but did not refer specifically to the question of the divorced and remarried. *Katolsk Orientering*, Nr. 8, 23 April 2003.

23 Timothy Buckley CSSR, *What Binds Marriage*, p. 124.

24 See chapter two.

25 East Anglia.

26 Laura Shahani, 'Working Paper on Family for the Diocesan Synod', Chennai, India, March 2003 *in Just Between Us*, Newsletter of the Bethany Family Institute, vol. 3, Issue 2, April 2003, pp. 6–7.
I am indebted to Mrs Catherine Richardson of *Catholic Marriage Care* for supplying the information about the *CMC* training.

27 See chapter four.

28 See chapter eight.

29 *Catechism of the Catholic Church*, § 1617.

30 See chapter five.

31 *Catechism of the Catholic Church*, § 1651.

Chapter Twelve

Regaining Integrity

*There are lots of things I would have chosen to do differently
today, but ... I can't go back and say let's make this choice
another choice ... What's important to me now is ... to move on
and hope that people will see me for the person I am.*
Crown Princess Mette-Marit of Norway[1]

When we communicate, I feel like a whole person.[2]
Crown Prince Haakon of Norway to his bride, Mette-Marit

A young Roman Catholic man, working in television, recently
made a programme about Catholicism as he saw it. He
included an interview with a Benedictine monk and,
inevitably, the conversation turned to sexual morality and
particularly living together before marriage. The monk said
that the gift of self in the act of love was the most any man
and woman could give each other. It therefore seemed a pity
to give it in circumstances that did not include that lifelong
commitment. The young man smiled ruefully, saying, obviously referring to his own experience 'It's a bit late for that'.
The monk said that he had made a general statement, that he
was not out to judge anyone and then the conversation moved
on to other topics.

The young man's rueful smile seemed to show that he
thought that there was nothing he could do to change the situation now. His reaction reflected the notion, still lurking in the
hearts of many people, that once someone has lost his or her
virginity, there is no way back. As we have seen in earlier

chapters of this book, spiritual virginity is far more important than physical virginity and it is certainly possible to give the gift with its full meaning, also for someone who has given it without that meaning earlier in life.[3] This 'beginning again' reshapes the whole person, so that in a very real sense he or she regains virginity and the ability to give the gift of self in total integrity.

In this chapter I want to look at some examples of people who have regained their integrity ('wholeness'), both in our own times and in the past. It therefore describes the counterpart to the fragmentation ('being broken apart') through separating sex from lifelong commitment that we considered in chapter four.

Reintegrating the Gift

As we have seen, it is possible to redeem the gift of self by reintegrating it into married life and I have come across two particularly striking examples of women who have done just that.

Norwegian Crown Princess

Everybody loves a fairytale, especially the 'happily ever after' with which so many childhood stories end. Even though most of us know that life tends to be more complex than that, the wish for everything to come right in the end expresses a very deep seated human longing. That is why we like reading about 'Prince Marries Poor Girl', or even 'Prince Loves Girl from Problematic Background and Overcomes Objections to Marriage'.

A few years ago the Norwegian Crown Prince Haakon married a girl, Mette-Marit, who had, by any standards, had a very difficult early life. She had been involved with drugs and had a young son whose father had also been on drugs. Mette-Marit ended up raising the boy on her own and, having left the drugs scene, created a good home for him. At this stage in her life, she met the Crown Prince, they fell in love, and after much initial opposition from the King and Queen, the two of them were married in the Cathedral in Oslo, with Mette-Marit's son as a page boy. It does indeed sound like a fairytale and, if televised wedding pictures are anything to go by, they looked as if they loved each other very much. This is a story 'of our time': they lived together openly before the wedding and in that sense did not provide a complete example for others to follow. But nevertheless, she had come a long way from the degradation of drug taking and the gift of self outside a committed relationship. I cannot help seeing her acceptance of the child she found herself to be carrying (she could probably have had an abortion) and the way she had brought up that child on her own as signs of the person she really was. That was the person who inspired Haakon's love and enabled her to commit herself in marriage to him. At their wedding the Bishop of Oslo said that she had set an example by the way she had cared for her child as a single mother. He also said that God allowed us to make a fresh start.[4] This new beginning has blossomed further through the birth of the couple's first child, a daughter, who will in due course inherit the throne from her father.[5]

Marriage in White

When I discussed this book with a friend of mine, she told me about a woman who had made such a new start from an even more difficult background. June (not her real name) had been a prostitute, but had become a Christian and had changed her whole way of life. She met a man who came to love her and wanted to marry her. It was at this point that she realised the full extent of the healing that had taken place within her. As the wedding approached, she felt that God was inviting her to marry in white, with its symbolic significance of purity. For her, and her husband-to-be, the acceptance of this invitation meant that she had in a very real sense regained her virginity, so that she could now give herself to him, untouched.

John Donne

It has been much more difficult to find an example of a young man who has turned from a life of promiscuity to becoming a faithful husband, but the early seventeenth-century poet John Donne was, by all accounts, just such a man.[6] Donne is known for his distinctive and often difficult love poetry as well as for the 'Holy Sonnets' (love poetry addressed to God) that he wrote later in life and the sermons he preached as Dean of St Paul's, London.

Donne had not always thought himself destined for the Church, nor had his early life pointed to a future as a faithful husband. When he looked back on his marriage in later years, be saw God's hand in rescuing him

> . . . from the Egypt of lust, by confining my affections . . .

so that he was able to love one woman faithfully.[7] God had called him out of the 'Egypt of lust', just as he had rescued the Israelites from slavery in Egypt, to lead them to the Promised Land. After the premature death of his wife, Ann More, Donne composed a sonnet containing these lines:

> Here the admyring her my mind did whett
> To seeke thee God; so streames do shew their head;[8]

Both quotations make it clear that Donne saw his ability to love one woman faithfully both as a gift and a call from God. But the call came at a price, as the marriage to Ann More against the wishes of her guardian, who was also Donne's employer, led to the collapse of his promising career in public service. After his dismissal Donne was forced to look in other directions, which eventually led to a new life and call within the Anglican Church. Thus the two 'streams' of his human love and his love of God had their 'head' or source in the God who had called him to both.[9]

Regaining Integrity: Gospel Accounts

There are no Gospel accounts which directly tell us of a man or woman becoming a faithful husband or wife after having once led a dissolute life. On the other hand, one would surely be right to think that the lost ('Prodigal') son, whose story was told in chapter five, was so completely healed after his return home that he would also have regained the integrity necessary to become a faithful husband.

Can something similar not also be said about the woman who came to pour costly ointment over the feet of Jesus, while she was weeping and wiping her tears from his feet with her hair? The woman had a bad name in the town and the people who were with Jesus at the time were shocked that he let her approach him. But Jesus saw the love and the total repentance in all the woman's actions and he said to her,

> Your sins are forgiven ... Your faith has saved you; go in peace.[10]

We are not told what happened to the woman later or whether she ever married, but the words Jesus spoke to her surely healed her broken integrity and they are words each one of us can take to heart, whatever our need for healing.

Integrity and Temptation

The wish to give oneself, with integrity, in faithful married love does not stop a man or woman from experiencing sexual attraction in the 'wrong' circumstances. For someone trying to integrate all sexual feelings within one loving relationship this can be both disturbing and confusing. If such a person thinks that the temptation which goes with the feelings is a sin in itself, then that can lead to a sense of hopelessness, which, in its turn, may destroy all his or her good intentions.

The difficulty is increased in our times, because the pull of sexual attraction is often described as leading inevitably to a sexual act. I once read a novel in which a woman was described as being 'helplessly aroused', so that (according to the author whose name I have forgotten), she could do nothing except let her arousal run its course by engaging in an act of intercourse. The implication was that she had no real choice, nor did the man she was with.

Neither reaction helps the person concerned towards an integration of their sexual feelings. In the first case he or she overlooks the fact that temptation and sin are not the same thing: they may resist the temptation, but with an uneasy, even guilty, feeling that it should not have occurred at all. ('I must be a bad person to have such thoughts.') If, as in the second case, the people involved think they have no real choice in matters of sexual attraction, then the teaching of Christ in this respect not only appears unreasonable, but also fails to take account of reality.

The true reality, however, is that temptations present us with a choice, to yield or not to yield, and we are not alone when facing that choice. Christ himself was tempted in all things, but did not sin,[11] so that he knew, and knows, what it is like to be tempted, precisely in all things. In his strength it is therefore possible to turn away from sexual temptation too, so that, for those called to marriage, our whole being can be integrated into the complete gift of self in the act of love.

Individual Circumstances

In spite of what I have just said, there can be circumstances, for example due to childhood experiences, which can make it almost or totally impossible for some people to resist particular temptations, at any rate for a time. In a family where having affairs is taken for granted, the children cannot be expected to know that this is wrong. It may take years before they understand the full meaning of the act of love and it is only then that they can begin to take responsibility for the circumstances in which they give themselves. The gift outside marriage remains a sinful act, but an act for which the individual may not be fully responsible. I am reminded of what a confessor once said to me, when I wept over 'spilt milk', 'What could you actually have done *at the time*?' He was also implying, of course, that I had grown since then![12]

A Reply to the Young Man

What would I say to the young television reporter, who was, in a sense, also weeping over spilt milk, or perhaps, in his case, spoilt footage? I cannot say that it is possible to rewind the tape of his life and cut the footage that he now wished was not there. But it is possible to begin a new story from where he is now, as many people have done before him. One can even speak of 'fortunate faults' in some people's lives, 'fortunate', because the faults led them from fragmentation to the point where they were able to give themselves complete and whole, with full integrity. The young man does not need to rewind his tape, only to begin from where he is now.

Summary

This chapter shows that anyone can regain integrity in sexual behaviour and hence the ability to give oneself fully to a husband or wife, regardless of previous history. The chapter demonstrates how integrity may be regained by providing examples from real life and from the Gospels.

Further Reading

Karol Wojtyla (Pope John Paul II), *Love and Responsibility*, Collins Fount Paperbacks, 1982, 'Mystical and Physical Virginity', pp. 249–55.

David L. Edwards, *John Donne, Man of Flesh and Spirit*, Continuum London and New York, 2001, esp. pp. 244–98.
The book provides a fascinating account of Donne's personal development and includes reproductions of telling series of portraits made at various stages throughout his life, p. 178ff.

Notes

1 Interview in *The Times*, 13 July 2001 on the announcement of her engagement to Crown Prince Haakon.
2 Wedding speech as reported in *The Times*, 27 August 2001.

3 See especially chapter five.
4 *The Times*, 22 January 2004, 27 August 2001.
5 BBC News World Edition, 22 January 2004, http://news
.bbc.co.uk/2/hi/europe/3419745.stm
6 I am indebted to Professor Margaret Spufford for this helpful
suggestion.
7 John Donne, *Essays in Divinity* (ed.) Evelyn M. Simpson,
Oxford 1952, 75 [*sic*]. See also John Carey, *John Donne, Life,
Mind and Art*, new edition, Faber and Faber, London and
Boston, 1990, p. 59. (First published by same, 1981).
8 *The Poems of John Donne*, (ed.) Sir Herbert Grierson, London,
Oxford University Press, 1969, (first published 1933), Holy
Sonnets XVII.
9 David L. Edwards, *John Donne, Man of Flesh and Spirit*, pp.
244–98.
10 Lk 7:49, 50.
11 Heb 2:18.
12 This question has been discussed from a different angle in
chapter five.

Chapter Thirteen

In the Resurrection

... when they rise from the dead, men and women do not marry;
no, they are like the angels in heaven.

Mark 12:25

Love never comes to an end.

1 Corinthians 13:8

While I was preparing to get married, I talked to a Catholic layman, very happily married, about what would happen to married love in the Resurrection. Like many people who love, I felt that my love must last forever, and for me that meant beyond death. My friend said that he felt sure that every love worthy of the name would continue in eternity and his words encouraged me to believe that my 'I will' would have a meaning, even after my death.

This belief is supported by St Paul's words about love never coming to an end, yet Christ has made it clear that marriage as we know it does not continue after death and in the Resurrection men and women will not marry. We know very little about life after the Second Coming of Christ and the General Resurrection, but let us reflect on what we do know and try to draw some conclusions about the love of men and women who have been married in this life.

Christ and Mary in the Resurrection

In this book we have concentrated on the meaning of the physical gift of self between husband and wife, man and woman. It therefore seems natural to begin this section by considering what we know about the bodies of men and women in the Resurrection. The first thing that comes to mind is that, for the risen Christ, the physical reality of the Resurrection already exists. Catholics also believe that his mother Mary was taken up into heaven, body and soul, through the saving power of Christ.[1] We therefore know that there is a male and a female body, 'in the Resurrection'. Christ and Mary are types, or prophetic images, of what we will all become as men and women who will, in a real sense, continue the life we now know.

Christ's Resurrection Body

We know from the Gospels that Christ appeared to his followers after his Resurrection and that he was the man of flesh and blood whom they had known and who had been crucified and died. He was also the man they met on the road to Emmaus after he had risen and who cooked fish for them on the banks of the Sea of Tiberias.[2]

St Luke tells us how some of the disciples meet Christ on their way to Emmaus, a village near Jerusalem. They do not recognise him, but, after talking to him on the way, they press him to go with them and share their evening meal. As he breaks bread with them, they are able to recognise him, after which he vanishes from sight. Later they meet up with the Apostles in Jerusalem and again Christ appears to them. Seeing their fear (they think he may be a ghost), he says to them,

> Why are these doubts stirring in your hearts? See by my hands and my feet that it is I myself. Touch me and see for yourselves; a ghost has no flesh and bones, as you can see I have.

He then shows them his hands and his feet and asks if they have anything to eat. They offer him a piece of grilled fish, which he eats in their presence.[3] Christ demonstrates to them both that he has a real body, because ghosts do not eat, and that that body is the same as the one that was killed on the Cross, as the nail marks show. It is therefore a body that has been shaped by his life on earth or, as the Catechism puts it, 'Christ is raised with his own body'.[4]

On the other hand, there is a difference between the physical reality of Christ's body before and after the Resurrection. One could say that the Risen Christ lives in another dimension, so that he is able to appear through closed doors and grant or withhold recognition. The commentary to the *Jerusalem Bible* states that, while Christ's body retains its identity, it is modified in a way that prevents the disciples from recognising him, until he has given them a sign, which opens their eyes.[5] It is a spiritual body.

What is more, there is identity not only of Christ's body, but of his whole person, including the experiences and relationships of that person before death. The risen Christ relates to his disciples in a way that builds on what went before and they respond to him in ways that depend on how close they had been to Christ before his death and Resurrection.

It is significant that it is John, who was closest to Christ and who followed him to the Cross, who recognises him first. When he and Peter and some of the other disciples are returning to shore on their fishing boat and see a man on the shore, John is the first to recognise him as Jesus. 'It is the Lord', he says. At which the impetuous Peter leaps into the water to swim ashore.[6]

Peter longs to see Jesus, but he is also weighed down by awareness of his denial of the Lord before the Crucifixion, ('I do not know this man'[7]). Jesus is well aware of this and gives Peter a new chance, 'Do you love me?' he says, and when Peter replies, 'Yes, Lord, you know I love you', Christ repeats the question two more times, thereby blotting out Peter's triple denial of him.[8] In other words, Jesus' relationship with Peter after the Resurrection is in direct continuity with the friendship that had gone before.

Christ did not only appear to his male disciples. It is in

keeping with his respectful attitude to women (revolutionary to his contemporaries, but as it was meant to be, 'from the beginning') that his first Resurrection appearance is to Mary of Magdala, whom he had cured of serious illness.[9] It is also in keeping with her deep gratitude to him, and the closeness she must have felt to him, that she is among the first (also women) to go to the grave after Jesus had been laid there. Together with the other women she is sent to bear the Good News of his Resurrection to the (male) disciples. Thus Christ's friendship with both men and women continues beyond the Resurrection, and, we must believe, in eternity.

Christ's Resurrection body has the same identity as the body that was crucified, but Christ's body did not decay. For us it will be different, as our bodies will not rise immediately after we die – unless we die very close to the Second Coming. However, since our Resurrection bodies will, like that of Christ, be fully human and therefore individual (no two people are the same), we must believe that our new bodies will be shaped by the lives we have led in our 'old' bodies. This means that our new bodies will bear the imprint of all our loving actions, including the acts of love in which we have given ourselves to our spouses.

St Paul describes in beautiful words the change that will happen to all human beings when Christ comes again, whether they are living or dead at that time:

> We are not all going to fall asleep [i.e. die], but we are all going to be changed, instantly, in the twinkling of an eye ... The trumpet is going to sound, and then the dead will be raised imperishable, and we shall be changed, because this perishable nature of ours must put on imperishability, this mortal nature must put on immortality.[10]

Our bodies will be changed, but we will still be the men and women we had become at the end of our lives, now living in eternity.

Mary's Resurrection Body

The Assumption of Mary, body and soul, into heaven after her death, follows from the fact that she is the Mother of God.[11] Because she was to become the Mother of God, she was, by the power of Christ, conceived without Original Sin. Therefore her body did not have to decay, but was 'taken up into glory'.[12] The words 'taken up into' are important, since they translate the Latin-based 'assumption'. Christ 'ascended', he 'rose' from the dead, but Mary was 'taken up', she was 'assumed' into heaven.

The Mary now living in her 'Resurrection body' is the Mary of Nazareth who said 'yes' to God's call to become the mother of his Son and she is the Mary who gave birth to and brought up her Son Jesus.[13] She is also the Mary who stood at the foot of the Cross and who, after the Resurrection, prayed with the disciples for the coming of the Holy Spirit over the Church.[14] I have no doubt that all these events left their marks on her face and have found expression in the appearance of her glorified body.

'When They Rise from the Dead, Men and Women do not Marry'[15]

Since we have before our eyes of faith the Resurrection bodies of Christ and Mary, male and female, we also have a pattern of what we will be like when we rise from the dead as men and women of spirit and flesh, created for eternal life.

The question of how men and women would relate to each other in the Resurrection was already under debate in the Jewish community at the time of Christ. What would happen 'in the Resurrection' to someone who had been married more than once? Members of a Jewish religious group called the Sadducees (who did not believe in the Resurrection) put the extreme case of a seven-times-married woman to Christ. Who would she be married to in the general Resurrection? In reply, Jesus says that when they rise from the dead, men and women do not marry, and then he adds that they are as the angels.[16] How are we to understand that?

Angels

Angels are spiritual beings, each with an individual personality. Like us, they have intelligence and free will, but, unlike us, they do not have bodies.[17] Being like the angels after our resurrection therefore cannot mean that we will be pure spirit, nor that the male-female complementarity will be lost, since a man and a woman, Christ and Mary, already live 'in the Resurrection', as forerunners for us all. In what ways, then, can we be like the angels after we have risen from the dead?

After the general Resurrection the whole of Creation will be complete, because all God wanted to say through men and women, created in his image, will have been said. In the words of John Paul II:

> It is the *quantitative* closing of that circle of beings, who were created in the image and likeness of God, in order that, multiplying through the conjugal 'unity in the body' of men and women, they might subdue the earth.[18]

Men and women will be like the angels in that they will not have children, but they will also be like them in another sense, which, in my view, is more significant. The *quantitative* circle has been completed, but the word implies that there is also a *qualitative* circle in which our life with God and each other will continue to grow, so that we must imagine an ever-expanding circle, indeed a 'circle' without bounds. Life within that 'circle' will be like that of the (faithful) angels in that all the people in it will have let themselves be filled with God's overflowing and patient love. In this perfect communion of male and female persons, there will be an intimacy which will not destroy the individuality of each human being, 'but rather will make it stand out to an incomparably greater and fuller extent'.[19] We will therefore be more ourselves, but what will happen to the love between husband and wife in the absence of sexual intimacy? To put the question differently, 'Why does marriage have to be for this life only?'

Marriage and the Church: A New Creation

As we have seen, the likening of the mutual gift of self in marriage to that of Christ to the Church must not be pushed too far, yet it throws light on the nature of the self-giving of Christ and on the response we are all invited to give to him. Marriage is the most obvious and immediate way of giving oneself to another. At a different level, this is the kind of fidelity which Christ lived out during his life on earth, which he goes on living during the time of the Church, and which will be perfected in what could be called the 'Resurrection Community', after his Second Coming.

How can we make ourselves ready for life in this future Community? We prepare for our ultimate future during every moment of our present lives, because all these moments are rooted in our sharing in the life of Christ. Married couples come to love each other with Christ-like love, specifically through the sacrament of matrimony, but, through the liturgy, they also share in the life of Christ in union with everyone in the Church. The high point of this union is expressed in the celebrations of Maundy Thursday, Good Friday and the Easter Vigil, when we follow Christ from the 'wedding' joy of the Last Supper, through the suffering of the Crucifixion to the renewed joy of his Resurrection.[20] At all these liturgies, and indeed at every Mass, the Church responds with ever growing fidelity to Christ's gift of himself. What is more, as we have already seen, the mutual gift of husband and wife in marriage is taken up into the union between Christ and the Church. Like that union, marriage points beyond the time of the Church to the Second Coming, when it will be transcended by a new way of sharing in the life of God.

Widening Perspectives

As I see it, the preparation of fallen mankind for the final Coming of Christ at the end of time has always involved a widening of perspectives and an ever greater inclusiveness, until the 'circle' of human beings, mentioned above, is finally complete. That fulfilment has been, and is being, prepared for during the time of the Old Testament, the New Testament and, finally, during the time of the Church, in which we now live.

We are reminded of God's will to save all men and women every time we hear the words of the Eucharistic Prayer of the Mass praise God the Father, because,

> Even when [man] disobeyed you and lost your friendship
> You did not abandon him to the power of death,
> But helped all men to seek and find you.
> Again and again you offered a covenant to man,
> And through the prophets taught him to hope for salvation.[21]

The biblical account of how God began to lead mankind back to himself, begins with the call of Abraham to leave his own city of Ur (in what is now Southern Iraq) to set out for a country which God would show him. The country was to be populated by Abraham's descendants, and both country and people would later be called Israel.[22] In obedience to God's will, Abraham set out, with his wife and household, towards the Promised Land and so, eventually, became the Father of the Chosen People. Thus the call of one man led to the call of a whole people.

The prophets told Israel to expect a saviour and the whole of the Old Testament in various ways points to the coming of this saviour. But, just as Abraham was told to set out without knowing where he was going, so Israel was asked to expect a saviour, without being told the nature of this saviour. The Israelites were simply to trust in God and wait for what, or rather, *who* would come.[23] The Eucharistic Prayer just quoted reminds us of the next, and wholly unexpected, act in the 'drama' of Salvation,

> Father, you so loved the world
> That in the fullness of time you sent your only Son to be our
> Saviour.[24]

God was to send his own Son Jesus as Saviour to his People, so that, again, the movement is from one person to a whole people, but this time the call of the Chosen People was only the beginning of a wider call. God's self-revelation in Jesus Christ was carried beyond the People of Israel (who, *as a People*, rejected their Saviour) to everyone willing to believe, so that a new People of God was formed, which is the Church. The pattern before us is therefore one of a continued widening of boundaries, from the one God-man Jesus, to the Israelites, to the Church and, through the Church, to everyone through the ages. At the same time there is a deepening of the closeness between God and his People to the extent that the Church can be called the Bride of Christ, as we have seen.[25]

In our own times, the Church has become increasingly aware that everyone who acts according to the mind of Christ is in fact a follower of Christ, whether he or she knows it or not.[26] Again we see the widening of the number of those who can be said to belong to Christ.

It is not surprising that, at the end of time, the Church itself should open up in a new and grace-filled way, when Christ comes in splendour and there will be a New Heaven and a New Earth, filled with those who have risen from the dead.[27] At that time, even the potentially all-inclusive community of the Church will no longer be needed, because God will be 'all in all' and no one, who has not deliberately chosen this, will be a stranger or an outsider.[28]

It is against this background that the 'no marrying' in the Resurrection must be seen. Marriage is of necessity exclusive. It is between this particular man and this particular woman and their gift of self in the act of love belongs to them only. However open they are to other people, their mutual self-giving has to be for them alone. Just as the Church will cease to exist, but its members will be opened up to a fuller, God-filled communion, so marriage will no longer exist, but those who have been married will come to share in the life of God in a way that includes all that was good in their marriage (or marriages) on earth. There are two aspects of marriage which point with particular clarity to the nature of our Resurrection life: openness and spontaneity.

Openness

In a good marriage there is an experience of openness to the other person, which is linked closely with the act of love. Marriage has the potential to bring a couple to the point where nothing is hidden, in any area of their lives. Such openness means that they have truly become part of each other and see each other as they really are. It is as if they inhabit a world where fear of being judged has been replaced by a trusting openness, in which each is free to be totally the selves they were created to be.

Spontaneity

Being oneself is closely linked with the ability to be spontaneous. As we have seen earlier, the word spontaneous comes from the Latin *sponte*, which means *voluntarily*, that is, of one's own free will.[29] At its best, acting spontaneously can be accompanied by an immense sense of freedom, so that someone might say, 'When I did this, I was completely myself.' Often a spontaneous action involves reaching out to another person, touching them or embracing them, and, for a Christian, such spontaneity can be experienced as a prompting by the Holy Spirit.

Nowhere do men and women more profoundly want to act spontaneously than when they make love, and nowhere is it more difficult. Helen and Luke, in the novel we looked at in chapter six, sought release from the problems of their relationship by making love, but their lovemaking did not fully take into account any future they might have together and what commitment they had to each other. It was a gift 'of the moment' rather than a gift for life. They might have said that they acted spontaneously, but it was a wounded spontaneity. In a marriage husband and wife also want to act spontaneously in their lovemaking and it is one of the arguments against Natural Family Planning that the couple cannot act 'spontaneously'. But a spontaneity, which is anchored in the will to do right, takes into account the whole truth about those involved. Such an ability to be spontaneous can be achieved only with the help and grace of God, but even so, it can only be a foretaste of the total freedom and integration of the Resurrection.

When we rise from the dead, we will be set free in a way which I would associate with that prompting of the Spirit which at times moves us to a completely truthful spontaneity, even in our present lives. This is a precious, if distant glimmer of how our Resurrection bodies will be guided by that same Spirit.[30] Can we, in a similar manner, catch a glimpse of what will happen to the Christ-like love between husband and wife, when we rise from the dead? I think we can.

It is Fulfilled

The act of love seals a marriage and makes it irrevocable. Giving ourselves in this way is the most we can give to another human being, yet married love transcends even this profound physical expression. There are many circumstances in which this love cannot be shown through a sexual act, because of illness, for instance, or in old age. But that does not mean that love ceases to grow. Husband and wife have handed themselves over to each other through their vows and the act of love, but even in bodies that are no longer capable of this act, they continue the gift of one person to the other, and, as they grow older, the gift becomes ever more spiritualised.[31] I still remember the look of profound love I once saw between a particular husband and wife as an example of how much can be said with a single glance.

Can the growth of love, even when bodies cannot express it in a sexual act, not point to the way in which love will be expressed, 'in the Resurrection', when there will be no marriage? It seems to me that the depth of mutual self-revelation that happens between a husband and wife, who love each other, must continue in eternity, because it carries within it the image of God's own self.

Consummation

For married couples, the consummation of their marriage, which they have lived out during their time on earth, will be taken up into the final consummation of Christ's love for the Church at the Second Coming. It will find its place in that communion of love, in which everyone who has sought to do what is right will share. It will be a place, which can be taken only by the love of this particular man and this particular woman.

Thus, the way we love on earth, and the way we give ourselves, husband to wife and wife to husband, will shape not only that life, but our lives in eternity, because 'male and female he created them', in his image and likeness, as gift for each other in love.[32]

❦

At the end of time, at the wedding feast of Christ, all real love will be celebrated and all who have said 'yes' to Christ during their lifetime, those called to marriage and those called in other ways, will add their 'yes' to that of the Church. With the whole Church they will respond to the question which Christ asked at his first Coming and which has resounded down the centuries of Time:

> Do you love me?
> Yes, Lord, I do.

Summary

In the Resurrection men and women do not marry, yet they will rise as men and women, presumably with the capacity, if not the wish, to make love. This chapter reflects on the relations between men and women in the Resurrection in the light of Scripture and spiritual writing.

Further Reading

John Paul II, *The Theology of the Body*, Pauline Books and Media, Boston 1997, pp. 238–49.

These pages reflect, profoundly, on the meaning of being male and female in the Resurrection.

Anita Dowsing, *A Marriage in Our Time*, Sheed and Ward, London 2000. A case study of a 'believer–non-believer marriage'; pp. 109–14 reflect on what will happen, in the Resurrection, to those who have done the will of God, without coming to faith.

Notes

1 *Catechism of the Catholic Church*, § 966.
2 Lk 24:13–43 and Jn 21:9–14. The 'Sea' or lake is still known by this name in Modern Israel.
3 Lk 24:38–43.
4 *Catechism of the Catholic Church*, § 999.
5 *The New Jerusalem Bible*. Note d to Lk 24:17. See also 1 Co 15:43–53 and note w to v. 44.
6 Jn 21:4–8.
7 Jn 18:15–27.
8 Jn 21:15–17.
9 Mk 16:9. The text literally says 'from whom he had cast out seven devils'. The Jerusalem Bible footnote on 'devils' or 'evil spirits' states that exorcisms frequently appear as cures of physical illness. (Mt 8:29).
10 1 Co 15:52–53. It is worth reading the context of this passage, under the heading 'The manner of the resurrection' in the *New Jersusalem Bible*, 1 Co 15:35–53.
11 Lk 1:35 and Sebastian Bullough, *Roman Catholicism*, Penguin Books, London, 1963, p. 154. Fr Bullough gives a particularly clear explanation of the development of Catholic doctrine on the role of Mary in the work of Salvation.
12 *Catechism of the Catholic Church*, § 966.
13 Lk 1:27–38, Lk 2:1–20 and Lk 2:51–52.
14 Jn 19:25–27 and Acts 1:14.
15 Mk 12:25.
16 Mt 22:30, Mk 12:25, Lk 20:35–36.
17 *Catechism of the Catholic Church*, §§ 329–330.
18 John Paul II, *The Theology of the Body*, p. 238. My emphasis.
19 Ibid., p. 242.
20 See chapter eight.

21 Eucharistic Prayer IV, *The Sunday Missal*, p. 45. I am indebted to Ruth Burrows for drawing my attention to the significance of this prayer in the present context.

22 Gn 11:31–12:2 and Gn 15:5–6.

23 See chapter two.

24 Eucharistic Prayer IV, *The Sunday Missal*, p. 45.

25 See chapter eight.

26 *Dogmatic Constitution on the Church (Lumen Gentium)*, in *Vatican Council II*, the Conciliar and Post conciliar Documents, (ed.) Austin Flannery, OP, Second Edition, seventh printing, Costello Publishing Company, New York 1984, §16.

27 Rv 21:5–8.

28 1 Co 15.28.

29 See chapter seven.

30 Ga 5:25.

31 John Paul II, *The Theology of the Body*, p. 244ff.

32 Gn 1:27.

Questions for Discussion

Chapter One

Name some ways in which the Catholic Church's teaching on marriage is relevant to people today.

Give some reasons why it might be more difficult for Catholics today to live church teaching on marriage and especially on sexual morality.

Name some arguments for and against co-habiting before marriage and discuss their advantages and disadvantages.

Chapter Two

Give some examples of people in the Bible who have had to do a lot of waiting in their lives. What effect did their waiting have on them?

Name some *kairos* moments in Scripture and in your own life or the life of someone you know.

Name some positive and negative aspects of waiting.

Chapter Three

A friend of yours is considering IVF treatment and praising its possibilities. How would you react?

What would you say to someone who told you that there is no such thing as absolute truth?

In your view, would a 'kneeling' attitude to scientific research mean that the scientist had stopped thinking for him or her self? Give reasons for your answer.

Chapter Four

What would you say to someone who says that the Catholic Church has a negative attitude to sex?

'Catholics are not expected to think for themselves'. Do you agree or disagree with this statement? Give your reasons.

Give an example from your own life of coming to understand your faith better.

Chapter Five

In what sense is the act of love a life-changing experience?

Describe in your own words the meaning of the act of love in marriage.

Why does the Church teach that the act of love belongs in marriage only?

Chapter Six

What would you say to someone who argued that you had to try out sexual compatibility before marriage?

In what sense is the biblical expression 'Adam knew Eve' an appropriate term for the act of love?

Give some examples of what you would consider to be the 'Holy of Holies' in someone's life.

Chapter Seven

Discuss the role of privacy in the expression of married love.

Does every couple have the necessary privacy not only for the act of love, but for being together as a couple?

A friend tells you that the Church's teaching on contraception is unrealistic. What would you say?

'The Church teaches that a couple must intend to conceive every time they make love.' Is that true? Give reasons for your answer.

Chapter Eight

It is easy for a woman to see herself as part of the Church, the 'Bride' of Christ, but how does this image work for a man?

What does the prostration of the clergy at the beginning of the Good Friday liturgy in the Catholic Church mean to you?

In what way can the fidelity of Christ to the Church help couples remain faithful to their marriage vows?

Chapter Nine

List some advantages and disadvantages connected with the high expectations of marriage today.

Give reasons why, in the teaching of the Catholic Church, a sacramental, consummated marriage is for life.

What reasons for being faithful to a marriage would you give to a person who says that he or she no longer feels anything for his/her spouse?

Chapter Ten

How would you explain the concept of nullity to a non-Catholic?

Describe a situation, where, in you opinion, a temporary separation between husband and wife could help the marriage to survive in the long term.

What meaning does the gift of self have in an irregular marriage?

Chapter Eleven

Why can it look to some people as if the Church considers sexual sin worse than any other sin?

What is Christ's attitude to sexual sinners that he met?

Name some arguments for and against people in 'irregular' situations receiving communion.

Chapter Twelve

What would you say to someone who wanted to give the gift of self with its full meaning, after an early 'wild' life?

In your experience, what attitudes can help or hinder someone who wants to begin again in this way?

Are men and women different, when it comes to regaining integrity?

Chapter Thirteen

In your view, why is marriage for this life only?

Since there will be no marriage in Heaven, what will happen, after death, to those who have been married in this life? Can their relationship survive?

How can a person who has been married more than once relate to those he or she has been married to?

General Information

Here are a few references that the reader may find useful. The bibliography below is very comprehensive.

Bibliography

Sexual Ethics Bibliography, compiled by James T. Bretzke, SJ, Jesuit School of Theology Berkeley, May 26 2002. Access via http://www.usfca.edu/fac-staff/bretzkesj/Sexual EthicsBibliography.pdf. An annotated bibliography.

Church Documents

Catechism of the Catholic Church, Geoffrey Chapman, London 1994.

Cherishing Life, Catholic Bishops' Conference of England & Wales, Catholic Truth Society, London 2004.
Life issues, including marriage and family life.

Deus Caritas Est, God Is Love, Encyclical Letter of Pope Benedict XVI, Catholic Truth Society, London 2006.
Part I includes teaching on married love. This document came out too late to be considered in the text of the present book.

Familiaris Consortio, The Christian Family in the Modern World, Apostolic Exhortation of Pope John Paul II, Catholic Truth Society, London 1981.

Gaudium et Spes, The Church in the Modern World, in Vatican Council II, The Conciliar and Post Conciliar Documents (ed.) Austin Flannery OP, New Revised Edition 1975, Seventh printing 1987.
§§ 47–52 deal with marriage and family life.

Books

John Paul II, *The Theology of the Body,* Human Love in the Divine Plan, Pauline Books and Media, Boston, 1997.
Contains addresses to general audiences on the Theology of the Body, 1979–1984, as well as the Encyclicals *Mulieris Dignitatem* 'On the dignity and Vocation of Women', *Evangelium Vitae* 'The Gospel of Life', and *Humanae Vitae* 'Of Human Life'.

Carlo Maria Cardinal Martini, *On the Body*, A Contemporary Theology of the Human Person, Crossroad Publishing Company, New York 2001.
Personal reflections on the meaning of the body, generally and in relation to marriage.

Christopher West, *The Theology of the Body Explained,* Gracewing Publishing, Leominster 2003.
——, *The Theology of the Body for Beginners*, Ascension Press, West Chester (USA) 2004.

The above two books are explanations of Pope John Paul II's *The Theology of the Body.*

Karol Wojtyla (Pope John Paul II), *Love and Responsibility*, Collins *Fount Paperbacks*, 1982. Also published by Ignatius Press, San Francisco, 1994.
An inspiring work on love between man and woman.

See also **Further Reading** at the end of each chapter.

Web Sites

Association of Separated and Divorced Catholics:
http://www.asdcengland.org.uk

Bishops' Conference of England and Wales:
General Web Site
http://www.catholicchurch.org.uk
Has menus on 'Issues and Info' and 'Faith and Life'. The latter has a link to the *Catechism of the Catholic Church* on the Vatican website.

'Listening 2004' Web Sites
Following the national consultation about marriage and family life 'Listening 2004' by the bishops of England and Wales, which was referred to in chapter one, a range of resources have been produced which can be accessed via the following web sites:

http://www.everybodyswelcome.org.uk
Resources for welcoming people in parishes and also for families in specific situations (e.g. handicapped member, believer-non-believer marriage, separated or divorced).

http://www.homeisaholyplace.org.uk
Resources on family spirituality.

http://www.passingonthefaith.org.uk
Resources to help parents and grandparents to pass on the faith.

Churches Together for Families:
http://www.marriage-preparation.co.uk
Ecumenical site on behalf of 'Churches Together for Families' aimed mainly at those involved in marriage preparation. Includes booklets for downloading and much helpful practical

information, including examples of Roman Catholic.- Anglican co-operation in (Anglican) diocese of Exeter.

Fertility UK
http://www.fertilityuk.org
Natural Family Planning and related issues.

Marriage Care (formerly Catholic Marriage Care):
http://www.marriagecare.org.uk
Offers counselling for those with marital or relationship difficulties as well as short courses for couples preparing for marriage. Also acts as a resource for parents and teachers responsible for sex education.

Marriage Encounter:
http://www.wwme.org.uk or http://www.wwme.org (World wide).
A movement of couples, priests and religious working for the renewal of the Church through the sacraments of matrimony and holy orders.

US Catholic Bishops' Website:
http://www.usccb.org

Vatican:
http://www.vatican.va
Encyclicals etc. can be downloaded from here.

www.ingramcontent.com/pod-product-compliance
Lightning Source LLC
Chambersburg PA
CBHW031253090426
42742CB00007B/442